THE Couch

BOOK

Finding and Buying the Couch of Your Dreams

FAYAL GREENE

CADER BOOKS/JOHN BOSWELL ASSOCIATES

HEARST BOOKS   NEW YORK

Library of Congress Cataloging-in-Publication Data

Greene, Fayal
    The couch book. Finding and buying the couch of your dreams / Fayal Greene.
        p.   cm.
    Includes index.
    ISBN 0-688-11363-X
    1. House furnishings—Purchasing. 2. Seating (Furniture)—Purchasing. 3. Furniture—Styles. I. Title
    TX315G74 1993
    645-4--dc20   92-36409
                                                                   CIP

Printed in Singapore
First Edition
1 2 3 4 5 6 7 8 9 10

DESIGNED BY NAN JERNIGAN / THE COLMAN PRESS

Acknowledgments

My greatest thanks go to Maia Javan for her diligent picture research and excellent eye. Paul Deutsch of Houston Upholstery Interiors, 39 West 19th Street, New York City, revealed the secrets of couch construction, and all of the decorators mentioned in Chapter 5 gave generously of their time and expertise. The manufacturers and retailers, large and small, sent precious photos promptly, and Melinda Florian Papp kindly shared information about a beautiful Georgian sofa. Denise Marcil, as always, was supportive even when she was right and I was wrong.

Contents

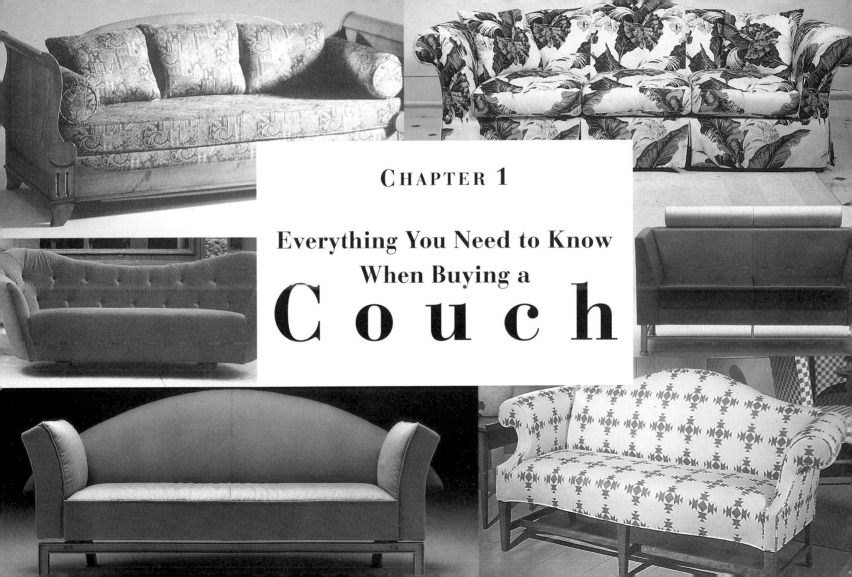

Chapter 1

Everything You Need to Know When Buying a
Couch

The thought of buying a couch is known to make strong, assertive people act like timid children. It's a commitment, and commitments can be daunting. A couch is BIG—a wrong choice will be there in the living room for all to see. A couch is expensive—few people can afford to simply replace mistakes on this scale. And a good couch lasts virtually forever with periodic reupholstery or slipcovering. This is only good if it's the right couch. There are literally thousands of couches on the market in all sorts of styles and coverings, making choosing the right one very confusing.

Everyone needs help in narrowing down those choices and finding out what their considerable financial commitment will buy. Most people buy their couches at retail, though some use decorators and a few brave or detail-obsessed souls find an upholsterer and have the sofa made to order. Fortunately for the American consumer, retail sources offer an enormous selection of serviceable and handsome upholstered furniture in a wide range of prices. This book provides help for both retail and custom buyers by providing reliable information on all aspects of choosing a couch, followed by a list of sources for furniture and information.

After deciding to buy a couch, the first task—and the subject of this chapter—is to assess priorities. Setting a realistic budget is essential. Fortunately, there are a surprising number of useful and attractive couches at all price levels. The room where the couch will sit should be sketched and measured to avoid unpleasant surprises when the couch comes into the house. Shopping checklists are useful to cut confusion and keep track of those all-important details while actually in the store.

Couch styles are covered in the next chapter. Furniture departments and specialty stores are filled with everything from ruffled Victorian settees to stark black-leather-and-chrome sofas. It's useful to look at a wide range of styles before making a final decision. Sometimes, rather than matching the style of other furniture or the architecture of the room, it can be very effective to mix shapes and periods. A traditional club sofa might make a modern room more welcoming, while a streamlined Deco couch could add glamour to conventional surroundings. A knowledge of style names makes communicating with furniture salespeople much easier and saves time.

It's also useful to know something about construction: what's under the upholstery and why some frames and fillings cost more than others. Chapter 3 tells "The Inside Story." Those often quoted but mysterious words, *"eight-way hand-tied springs"* and *"down-wrapped foam,"* actually describe highly regarded construction techniques. *Tufting* and *buttoning* aren't just decorative—they affect the comfort as well as the looks of a couch. Although the structural parts of a couch are hidden, a few simple tests can help to determine the sturdiness of an upholstered piece without actually taking it apart. All these factors contribute to the couch's comfort when reading, chatting or napping.

In Chapter 4 the very important subject of fabric to cover the couch is discussed; among other reasons, it's the upholstery that people notice first. Choosing a particular color or pattern can make the furniture seem longer, bigger or smaller. It can even give the impression of a different style. Fabrics differ widely regarding durability, design and cost; each weave, such as *brocade, damask, linen* or *repp,* has its particular characteristics. Certain materials are more appropriate for upholstery, others for slipcovers.

Part of selecting the right fabric involves a choice of skirt, arm and cushion details. Besides looking different, the same couch can require surprisingly different amounts of fabric yardage depending on these details as well as the size of the pattern *repeat.* Fabric requirements, of course, have a big effect on the total cost of the furniture. Slipcovers are an increasingly popular choice to re-cover or simply change the look of a couch. They can be inexpensive—especially if they're concocted from one of the handsome bed sheet patterns available in every store—or as expensive as reupholstery if fine damask and lots of custom details are used. Leather is an alternative upholstery material that is very expensive but extremely durable.

Because of the high cost of a fine couch as well as the many choices that need to be made, some people prefer to work with an interior decorator who, they believe, will make choices for them and add custom touches to distinguish this couch from all the others. Few people realize that most custom details are available from the big upholstered furniture manufacturers at a considerably lower cost. Chapter 5 explains many of those elegant "Tricks of the Trade." It is possible to create a truly individual couch by studying and making choices from the catalogs of detailing to be found in most good furniture stores. Pictures clipped from decorating magazines are a great

LA-Z-BOY

62-473 Temptation apartment sofa

12 yards

help, since they show finely detailed furniture in a room setting. Even when working with a decorator, it's wise to be clear about how the couch should look when finished. Time spent in preparation will pay dividends in satisfaction later.

It's quick and easy to update or freshen a simple couch with inexpensive accessories and imagination—which is free. Many leading designers have shared their ideas with the readers of this book so that retail buyers and do-it-yourself decorators can have access to the tricks of the trade.

After setting priorities and making choices, it's time to buy the sofa. The final chapter explains the many sources for couches and how they differ. National chains and department stores are just a few of the places to seek the perfect piece of furniture. Discounters often offer substantial price reductions in exchange for a little more work on the customer's part. Many decorators have opened shops where consumers can find both the merchandise and the stylistic advice once available only to private clients. A fearless, well-prepared customer may actually infiltrate "To the Trade Only" showrooms or find bargains in the heated atmosphere of the auction houses. A directory of furniture sources is provided to simplify the search for the perfect couch.

This book explains in detail all a prospective couch buyer needs to know to make a great choice. With the information here, the reader will know couches, literally, inside out.

SETTING PRIORITIES

~ Cost ~

The question of cost should be settled first, since a new couch can cost anywhere from $250 to well over $10,000. Antiques prices soar into the stratosphere, as does specially trimmed custom work. Even without a precise dollar amount in mind, it is wise to determine a price range. In this book, a tassel system indicates cost:

𝄞	$250 to $750
𝄞𝄞	$750 to $1500
𝄞𝄞𝄞	$1500 to $4000
𝄞𝄞𝄞𝄞	$4000 and up

Almost every sofa will come in a version for each budget level; the vast majority of ready-made couches fall in the 🖌🖌 or 🖌🖌🖌 category. Inevitably, compromises will be many in the 🖌 category, whereas anyone lucky enough to have a 🖌🖌🖌🖌 budget should have infinite choice. Custom detailing and expensive fabric may raise the cost of even a moderately priced sofa by hundreds of dollars—it's sensible to choose the best shape, buy it in a simple cover and dress it up later when the budget is bigger. To get the best value for the money, the wise consumer tries to live by this motto: NEVER PAY RETAIL. THINK DISCOUNT OR SALE.

∼ *Durability* ∼

One factor to consider when setting a budget is the length of time the couch must last. If it's for a first apartment, will it be worth the cost of moving it? Used couches don't sell for high prices but moving is very expensive. A cheap couch that will be replaced at the next house may be the most economical choice. This is a perfect situation for 🖌 furniture.

LEXINGTON

Bob Timberlake sofa

20 yards

🖌🖌🖌

∼ Size ∼

How many people will ordinarily sit on the new couch? In reality, it's unlikely that more than one person will sit on a love seat (up to 5 feet long) or more than two on a sofa (6 feet or longer), despite the fact that a 7-foot sofa is commonly called a three-seater. Where a wall is not long enough to accommodate a three-seater comfortably, furniture can often be rearranged so the couch is perpendicular to the wall or stands in the center of the room as a sort of divider. Two couches of moderate length, either at a right angle or face-to-face, are more practical and more flexible than one huge piece of furniture.

∼ Mapping the room ∼

Before starting to shop, make a plan of the room showing the best possible couch positions. Using square-ruled graph paper will make this task fairly simple: usually one square on the paper represents one foot. A helpful tool is a 9- or 12-foot stiff metal tape measure such as builders use to gauge large spaces. Draw the outline of the room and write in the overall measurements. Measure and mark the locations of windows, doors and any special features, such as a fireplace or supporting beam that protrudes into the room. One or two good positions for the couch will show up clearly; perhaps against a long wall or close to the warming glow of a fireplace. Mark the compass points roughly on the plan and, to prevent fading, avoid placing the couch under a south or east window where sun will fall on the fabric for much of the day.

Is the room to be used occasionally for sleeping? Nowadays sofa beds look exactly like regular couches except that they are usually deeper (front to back) and need a larger opening to get into the room. The space needed to open the bed should be marked on the plan.

When choosing the place for a couch, allow space for end tables if they will be part of the furniture. Check traffic patterns; people should be able to walk across the room without running into pieces of furniture.

Next, measure the access route by which the couch will be brought into the room (doors, elevators, stairways, halls and so on) and mark these

HENREDON

8960
sectional

32 yards

measurements on the plan. Choosing a sofa that will fit easily around tight corners or through narrow doors prevents the expense of hoisting an oversized one through a window or even returning it (for which there is always a charge). Only sofas that can be brought in with ease should be considered; the effect of a very long couch can be produced by using a sectional. Accurate measurements become important when the width of the couch and that of the doorway are

nearly equal; an inch can make all the difference when trying to move a piece of furniture into a room. Height is important too; it may be difficult to maneuver a 10-foot couch through turns in a hall with 8-foot ceilings leading to a door whose height is 6 feet, 9 inches.

This sample plan shows a living room of fairly standard dimensions: 13 by 19 feet. It has a fireplace and two windows on the north wall and a door surrounded by bookcases on the west.

Neither of these is a good place for the couch. The long wall across from the fireplace, on the other hand, has plenty of room for a sofa in the 13 feet between the doors and the bookcase. Another possibility, somewhat closer to the fireplace, is in front of the long window in the east wall. Fading from the morning sun should not be a problem, though the couch could be put two feet from the window to avoid both intense light and drafts.

After checking all the measurements, from the front door of the house to the elevator to the room itself, it is clear that the couch must be no wider than three feet front to back to fit through the narrowest opening, that of the apartment. A six-foot-long couch will be easy to move and will not block traffic in the room; a seven-footer could be used on the long wall. Once possible couch positions are marked in pencil, copy the plan and take it to the store along with a copy of the following checklist for each couch under serious consideration. Collect pictures and specifications so the details will stay clear in your memory.

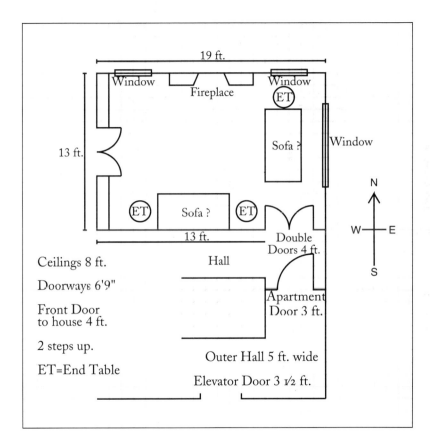

Checklist

Store _____

Name and/or number of couch _____

Manufacturer _____

Style _____

Comfort rating _____

Delivery date _____

Price _____

Dimensions

Length _____
Depth _____
Height _____
Extension (sofa bed) _____
Sketch of pieces _____
(sectional—the store should have this)

Filling and Construction _____

Cover material

Name _____
Number _____
Color _____

Special features

Arm covers _____
Extra pillows _____
Slipcover _____
Custom detailing _____

GLOSSARY

A number of words are commonly used to describe a piece of upholstered furniture that seats several people. Some have historical origins; others have regional roots. Most are interchangeable.

Couch A piece of furniture on which one or more may sit or lie down, usually upholstered. Includes divans, sofas and some beds. All of the terms below apply to couches.

Bench A long seat, usually made of wood or metal, accommodating several people. It may or may not have a back or arms, but is not normally upholstered. Loose cushions may be added for comfort

Davenport A rather old-fashioned word for a couch, especially a sofa bed.

Daybed A couch with one or two upholstered ends but at most a partial back support. Originally for napping, daybeds now substitute for sofas or even guest beds.

Divan A low, wide upholstered couch, usually without arms or back. From the Turkish word for an assembly room, extended to include its furniture.

Love seat A small couch on which two people can fit only by sitting very close together.

Sectional A couch in several segments which may be straight or curved and have one, two or no arms. The sections may be used in combination or separately as use and the shape of the room require.

Settee A bench or sofa; probably a form of the old word *settle*, a wooden bench with high arms and back to keep out drafts.

Sofa A couch with back and arms, generally completely upholstered.

THE KEY TO THE KEYS

Every couch shown in this book is keyed—a small chart beside the photo contains the information needed to find out what's on the market and what it costs. Knowing the exact specifications for each couch will help to narrow the multiplicity of choices by helping to identify suitable examples. The specifications apply to the couch as shown (it may be available in other sizes and fabrics which will require a different amount of yardage and will also affect the final cost):

MANUFACTURER

Name of couch (where applicable)

Fabric yardage required

Price range

In each case, the manufacturer's name is given. Although manufacturers who sell only to retailers will not sell directly to consumers, they do provide information numbers and are delighted to let the consumer know where to buy a specific piece of furniture. These numbers, which are to be found in the directory under FURNITURE MANUFACTURERS—RETAIL STORE SUPPLIERS, will also be useful in finding out about other furniture from the same manufacturer credited in a magazine article.

Other manufacturers sell only to the design trade. They are listed in the directory (Chapter 6) under FURNITURE MANUFACTURERS—TO-THE-TRADE Their furniture is normally sold in design center buildings that limit access to trade members, through whom consumers must go to buy the items. However, the directory entry about these showrooms lets you in on the secret that these places may be quite a bit more accessible than they want to appear.

The price ranges are indicated, within the limits mentioned on page 13. Not only do the measurements and choice of fabric affect the exact dollar price, cost may vary from store to store. It's always worthwhile to try to buy on sale or from one of the discounters also listed in the directory. The keys are invaluable to unlock the secrets of couch marketing.

CHAPTER 2

The Right
Couch

Right now in North America we have the biggest and, by any standards, the best selection of upholstered furniture in history. Dozens of large and hundreds of small manufacturers turn out couches in shapes and styles ranging from the ascetically simple to the hyperbolically baroque. What's more, almost without exception, these couches are built well enough to outlast their owners. Only the very cheapest unframed sofas are likely to fall apart—the rest have sturdy frames and durable fillings. Cost differences are due to refinements of structure and stuffing, richness of covering and exclusivity of design. These differences are covered in detail in this and the following chapters. A couch bought today can reasonably be expected to last a lifetime. It may be reupholstered or slipcovered when the fabric becomes soiled or outdated. But the couch goes marching on and repays for years the hours of thought devoted to choosing it.

The first and most basic decision in choosing a couch is: What style? The style is the underlying shape of the couch. Although the color or pattern of the upholstery fabric may change the appearance of a sofa (see Chapter 4), that underlying form is what determines the style. Over the years the most popular styles have undergone many variations and modifications. Nonetheless, the vast majority of couches belong to one of three styles.

Camelback

A hump in the center of the back distinguishes this style. There are two- or even three-humped versions, as well as reverse camelbacks with a dip in the center of the back.

PEARSON
1737-302
8 yards

Chesterfield

A couch with the arms at the same height as the back. The resulting sofa may look traditional or modern, depending on such details as the thickness and shape of the arms.

ATELIER INTL.
DUC sofa
21 yards

Club

Any one of the vast variety of couches with upholstered arms at a lower level than the back.

PEARSON
Multi floral chintz
12 yards

All of the other styles discussed are based on specific historical models; the three we've discussed have their roots in history, of course, but have proved so consistently popular that furniture makers have continued to develop and vary them for the last couple of centuries.

Although the styles as defined and illustrated here are quite well accepted in the design world, not every salesperson may know the names of all the styles in the store. In some localities style names may differ. Carrying a picture from this book or a magazine will make communication with salespeople easier.

ANTIQUE OR REPRO?

For lovers of a particular historic style, Chippendale or Art Deco for instance, isn't it better to find a real example than to compromise with a reproduction? Well, maybe not. Antique sofas, particularly eighteenth-century ones, have been fabulously expensive for a long time. Prices for twentieth-century "antiques" in popular styles, such as a sofa by Jacques-Emile Ruhlmann, the greatest of Deco designers, are rapidly heading for the stratosphere. Even for those lucky enough to have a fabulous budget, consider the following points.

1. Authenticity.

The frame of an old sofa may be rickety, the filling lumpy, the cover dingy. But if any of these elements is original, it is the duty of a collector to preserve it. The value of the piece lies in the vestiges of earlier times—but no one may be able to sit on an authentic treasure without helping to destroy it. This is obvious with very old pieces but actually just as true with newer ones

An English mid-Georgian (circa 1760) Chippendale camel-back mahogany sofa sold at Florian Papp Antiques for about $40,000 in the early 1990s.

2. Size.

Face it—we're considerably taller and, um, wider than our ancestors. Reproductions, while preserving the proportions and details, make allowances for these facts of life.

3. Styles.

Styles are not always what they seem. Early American, for instance, insofar as this is a style at all, is an invention of the furniture manufacturers of the 1950s. Actually, a genuine dark-stained maple settee with the original orange and brown print cover may be worth buying as a period piece of the future.

For use in a normal decorating scheme, the details of a Victorian or Regency sofa may be a bit intimidating—but they really can't be changed. With a reproduction there's more freedom. As grand an authority as Elsie de Wolfe, America's first professional interior decorator, said, "Better to buy a first-class reproduction than an inferior antique."

4. What about secondhand?

Many tales have been told of great sofas found at the Salvation Army for $15. In every show house living room he designed, the renowned decorator Arnold Copper included what he proudly referred to as his $60 ottoman. He found it at a yard sale. What he *didn't* mention was the $400 for retufting,

CENTURY
22-218 sofa
15.5 yards

plus the $250 for strengthening the frame, plus the seven yards of $100-a-yard fabric, plus the reupholstering cost!

On the other hand, a secondhand couch whose springs aren't sprung and whose frame doesn't wobble and whose stuffing doesn't smell like something died, is well worth buying. Maybe you can live with the orange upholstery. If not, turn to the slipcover chapter (page 127).

CAMELBACK

Before the time of design market weeks and trade magazines, furniture makers kept up with new styles by buying *pattern books* such as Thomas Chippendale's immensely popular *The Gentleman and Cabinet-Maker's Director*, published in 1754. These influential publications contain measured drawings of everything from footstools and couches to entire painted and paneled ballrooms. Chippendale's book showed many examples of

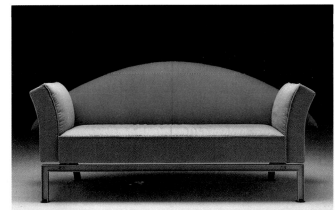

Left:

BAKER

McMillen Collection

18 yards

LIGNE ROSET

Antares sofa

12 yards

the *serpentine* or *camelback* sofa, an instant success that remains a basic couch style to this day.

Colonial American furniture makers inter-preted and adapted Chippendale patterns for well-to-do customers along the Eastern seaboard; during the Federal period the neo-classical and

HICKORY
CHAIR

1966-71
James River
Collection
9 yards

LEE
INDUSTRIES
3068 sofa
8 yards

is still among the most prized in the world today.

The camelback or serpentine back sofa has been extremely popular for at least 200 years and is still one of the three basic couch shapes (along with chesterfield and club sofas). The secret of its success is the graceful curve in the center of the back which has the power to make a large piece of furniture seem lighter yet charmingly formal. Several variations on the original shape have been devised over the years. Some sofas, like some camels, have more than one hump. Reverse camelbacks—with a dip rather than a hump in the center—are also popular.

Because this is such a universal shape, it does not demand any particular style of upholstery. Couches that echo the eighteenth-century Chippendale original designs have smooth, rather thin upholstery and long wooden legs that often are carved. Lots of skirted, overstuffed, sectional or pillow-heaped alternatives are available, however. The effect can range from cozy country to

French-inspired styles of the Adam brothers, Hepplewhite and Sheraton were all the rage. Duncan Phyfe of New York brilliantly translated these English designs into elegant furniture that

Donghia
San Marco sofa
20 yards

elegant drawing room to stripped-down contemporary. One of the great advantages of choosing this or one of the other standard and adaptable couch shapes is that the choice of fabric is unlimited, and a change of upholstery or even a slipcover can radically change the effect.

GRANGE

Camille three-seat sofa

17 yards

CHESTERFIELD

In the Victorian era of the nineteenth century, a favorite new sofa shape was the *chesterfield*, a deep-buttoned couch with the back and arms at the same height. One of the most comfortable pieces of furniture ever devised, the chesterfield is more popular today than ever—it's a favorite in rich leather for the ultimate men's club or bachelor apartment effect.

Left:

DRUXEL
HERITAGE

*1008-01
sofa*

22 yards

LIGNE
ROSET

*Salome
love seat*

12 yards

The original chesterfield relied on its deep buttoning for comfort rather than on the presence of cushions. It was usually covered in plush or tapestry. Today, besides leather, chesterfields are covered in everything from silk to denim. Variations on the chesterfield may have attached and/or loose cushions that sometimes completely disguise the underlying shape. A change of fabric or detailing can adapt the couch to a different room or an entirely new decorating scheme.

SWAIM
1152 sofa
15 yards

ATELIER
INTL.

*Cardigan
three-seat
sofa*

20 yards

ATELIER
INTL.

*Alter three-
seat sofa*

20 yards

JOHN
WIDDICOMB

*Mario
Buatta
Collection
Hanley sofa*

19 yards

CLUB SOFA

The *club sofa* is what most people seem to visualize when they hear the word "couch." Like the chesterfield, its roots go back to Victorian times. It's a fully upholstered piece of furniture whose arms are lower than its level back, unlike a chesterfield with arms and back at the same height or a camelback with its curved shape.

RJONES
Mansfield sofa

13 yards

SHELTON
MINDEL &
ASSOCIATES
FOR JACK
LENOR
LARSEN

*Arboretum
Collection
Hawthorn
sofa*

13 yards

The low soft arms of the club sofa give an open feeling; they are great to lean across or balance a book on. Possible variations on the club sofa shape are virtually unlimited. Cushions can be attached, loose or absent. Arms can be round, square or even cantilevered. The effect may be formal or totally unpretentious.

Absolutely any fabric from leather to chintz may be used to cover a club sofa, depending on how and where it will be used.

Century
22-960 sofa
19 yards

IKEA

910404
HOV two
seat-sofa

12 yards

RJONES
RJ sectional
13 yards

LEE
INDUSTRIES
3024 Sofa
17.5 yards

LA-Z-BOY

*61-333
Sierra sofa*

18 yards

MODERN ICONS

After World War I, a revolutionary modernism sprang from the German Bauhaus school of design. Architect-designers such as Marcel Breuer, Mies van der Rohe and Le Corbusier produced furniture that remains among the modern icons. Eileen Gray, an Englishwoman working in Paris, was also making architecturally shaped furniture that is still influential today.

Another revolution took place in 1981 in Italy, where a group of 20 architects and designers formed a group called *Memphis* (after the Bob Dylan song "Stuck Outside of Mobile with the Memphis Blues Again") to design furniture which has, so far, been more popular in Europe than in America. Ettore Sotsass and Bruno Magistretti are two of the founders of Memphis. French designers like Philippe Starck continue to make avant-garde furniture whose influence has yet to be felt in American popular style.

American designers and architects, too, enjoy designing signature furniture. Furniture galleries (many are listed in the back of this book) sell one- or few-of-a-kind architect sofas in their original form. Successful ones are copied for the mass market by various mainstream manufacturers. Each of the couches in this section was

designed by a famous architect or interior designer and has been illustrated endlessly in magazines and books. They are still being produced in their original proportions and materials. They are very popular with—surprise!—architects and interior designers and are always known by the name of their creator or the project for which they were created.

These couches are usually offered in the original covering materials. Because they are so

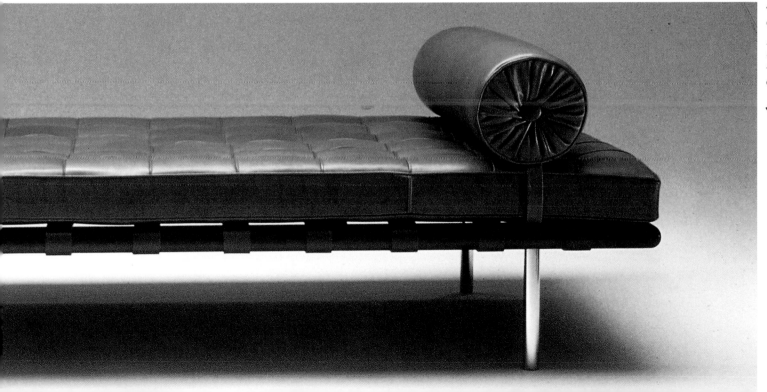

THE KNOLL GROUP

Mies van der Rohe sofa

6.5 yards

NEOTU

*Garouste &
Bonetti
Corbeille
sofa*

17 yards

well known and such design landmarks, attempts to change the upholstery usually look odd.

Design icons all *look* great, but some are more comfortable than others. Some people care more about how the couch looks than whether it's comfortable for a nap. You must sit and lie down on these couches to see how they fit. If you're a purist, these are for you. If not, look at some of the other categories for interpretations of these highly influential icons.

Despite the wide availability of innovative furniture, most people today choose traditionally styled couches—perhaps because a couch lasts so long. To the occasional despair of designers seeking a novel and distinctive effect, the tried and true sofa shapes provide the comfort most of

ATELIER
INTL.

*Le
Corbusier
LC/3*

9 yards

HERMAN
MILLER

*Nelson
sling sofa*

9 yards

us look for in a couch. Nonetheless, there are always people for whom the refined beauty of these examples of furniture as art transcends mere practicality.

I.L. EURO

Cappellini Anna Gili sofa

14 yards

ATELIER INTL.

Utrecht curved sofa

11.5 yards

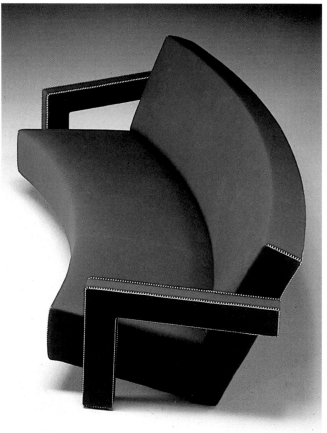

HERMAN
MILLER

*Eames sofa
compact*

11 yards

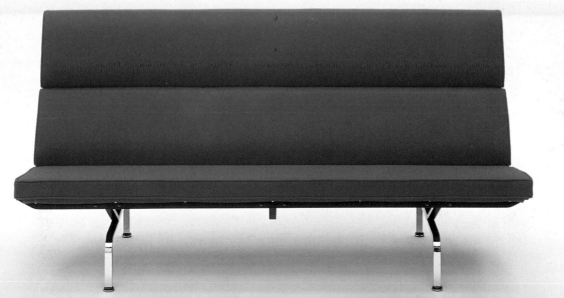

HERMAN
MILLER

*Eames soft
pad sofa*

17 yards

ARTS & CRAFTS, MISSION AND RUSTIC STYLES

At the end of the nineteenth century, Arts and Crafts designers from William Morris in England and Charles Rennie Mackintosh in Scotland to Frank Lloyd Wright and the Stickley brothers in the United States wanted to return to simple values and straight lines after the robber baron ethics and curlicued furniture of the Victorian era. Their straight-edged wood-framed couches are as much about politics as about design. All over England and America right-thinking people were sitting on upright plain-colored sofas whose wooden backs assured that they were nearly as uncomfortable (and as "virtuous" in the eyes of their creators) as the castle furniture of the Middle Ages. It's not too difficult to see why these designs are so very popular in the 1990s.

STICKLEY
89-291
Spindle sofa
8.5 yards

Highly influenced by Arts and Crafts furniture but much more cheerful is Mission furniture, which harks back to the Spanish era in early California. It combines straight lines with Western detailing. Oak was the wood of choice ("Solid as an oak!") for both Arts and Crafts and Mission furniture.

Some of these couches are more comfortable than others. Choose one with plenty of pillows between you and its straight sides or be prepared to sit bolt upright most of the time.

ATELIER
INTL.
Robie 3 sofa
8.5 yards

STICKLEY

*89-220
Prairie
settle*

8 yards

LANE

*1670-78
Grove Park
sofa*

13.5 yards

HICKORY
CHAIR

4809-73
sofa

8 yards

STICKLEY

89-208
Settle

8 yards

Away from cities, local craftsmen have for generations produced furniture using locally available materials but echoing the predominant styles of the day. Softwoods such as pine are roughly worked into tables and couch frames. Often the logs are rough surfaced; in some exam- ples the bark is left intact. In the Adirondacks, furniture is still made from thin flexible tree branches bent and woven into fanciful shapes. This is referred to as "twig" furniture, but its origins are in Arts and Crafts style.

LALUNE
603SM
settee
2 yards

Upholstery fabrics should echo the simplicity and rustic feeling of this furniture. Plain woven textures or simple stripes are most appropriate for Wright- and Stickley-inspired furniture; adaptations of Indian rugs and horse blankets can be found for Mission and rustic pieces. Leather, particularly in the light, natural colors of the old West, is another appropriate choice.

HaRry

*Club Easy
Cowboy sofa*

16 yards

Ligne
Roset

*Indian
Summer
sofa*

18 yards

EMPIRE AND BIEDERMEIER

Napoleon's idea of himself as a modern Roman emperor sent all of Europe on a classical kick in the first half of the nineteenth century. Ladies in high-waisted cotton dresses struck antique poses on daybeds or *chaises longues*. A Greek-inspired, double-ended couch (perfect for reclining) is named after a French beauty of the day, Madame Récamier. Round bolster cushions—thought to suggest classical columns—were

Left:

DREXEL HERITAGE

2266 daybed

11 yards

THAYER COGGIN

905-305 Biedermeier sofa

12 yards

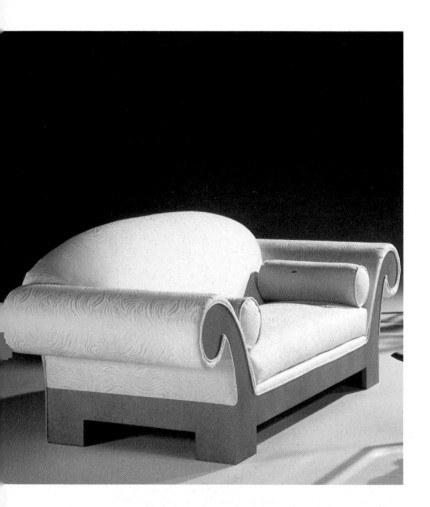

found on virtually every sofa everywhere. Even the democratic Americans fell in love with this French style, and American Empire couches are becoming more and more desirable to antiques collectors.

In Germany and Austria, the French imperial influence led, oddly enough, to a comfortable and solidly unpretentious middle-class style called *Biedermeier.* Sofas were framed in light-colored woods with graceful, simple curves and covered with plain or striped fabrics. Biedermeier's classic lines blend well with a variety of more assertive styles. Its emphasis on comfort makes it popular with people who resist formality but don't want a "country" look. Original pieces are becoming scarce and extremely expensive; excellent reproductions are being made to fill the demand.

Although Biedermeier couches are sometimes framed in dark wood, honey-colored maple or birch is more characteristic and youthful. American Empire pieces, on the other hand, were always made in dark woods, usually mahogany. To look their best, they should be surrounded by

THAYER
COGGIN
*905-303
Biedermeier
sofa*
10 yards

other "serious" pieces—they just don't have the lightheartedness of Biedermeier.

Upholstery for either style of couch should be quite plain. Solid-color woven textures or stripes in silk or horsehair (for *real* authenticity) are the materials to choose. Trim is usually limited to simple braid or cording.

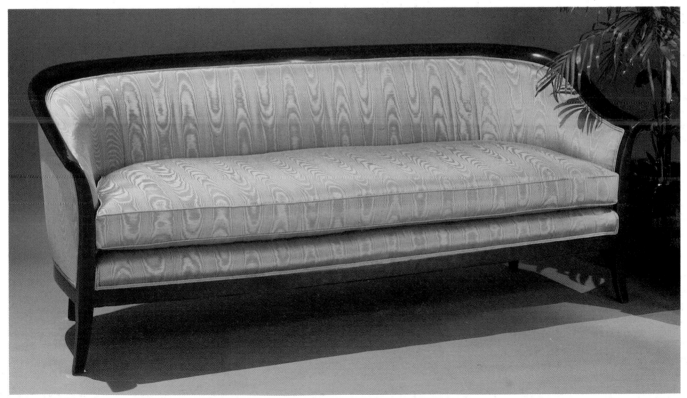

TROUVAILLES

Marienbad sofa

10.5 yards

FRENCH

"French Provincial" was a label for all sorts of good and bad country-style furniture some years ago—if it was French-inspired and formal, it was called "Louis." Provincial sofas had fruit-wood frames and flowery upholstery; Louis wore fake Aubusson in a pastel-painted frame with gilding and a tasteful touch of *ormolu*; gilded

Left:
PEARSON
1737-302 sofa
9 yards

CENTURY
22-987 sofa
14 yards

bronze decoration. Fortunately both of these very American "French" styles are now quite rare (collect them—they may soon become antiques!). They have been replaced by lighter-hearted, somewhat earthier furniture now produced by many manufacturers.

Light-colored wooden frames with softly curved and carved legs, arms and stretchers are characteristic of the style. If the wood is painted, the pastel color has usually been rubbed off so just a thin veil remains. The typical French couch today is really a settee—a cross between a bench and a sofa. The seat and sometimes the back are upholstered but the arms are wooden with at

JOHN WIDDICOMB

9063 French Collections sofa

9 yards

BRUNSCHWIG
& FILS
Brittany sofa
18.5 yards

most a little padded armrest. It's a charming, informal style best suited to country houses or informal rooms, such as kitchens and dens.

The typical fabric for French settees is classic *toile*—a graphic design in one color on natural cotton, often showing scenes from French country life—or a bright print from the Provence region of France. Any simple unpretentious cotton print such as ticking stripes could be substituted.

HENREDON

H8906
Natchez
love seat

16 yards

VICTORIAN

The late nineteenth century, even in Europe and America, is named for Britain's long-lived Queen Victoria. The monarch shared with the general public a taste for genteel but elaborate decoration—and lots of clutter. Comfort was most important; the newly invented coiled steel springs were covered with fat padding and tufting, making couches look as smug and

SWAIM
F 1080 sofa
19 yards

Left:
BAKER
Historic Charleston sofa
8.25 yards

well fed as the era's prosperous businessmen. Lush plush and velvet with heavy fringes made the upholstery resemble the stiff ball gowns of the era. For everyday use or in the country, however, heavy velvets and brocades were often covered by slipcovers in delicious flowered chintzes, many of which are still being produced.

Decorating details changed and evolved during the long Victorian era, but one or more comfortable, thickly upholstered couches were a necessary part of every drawing room. One of the most important sources of couch design was an illustrated pattern book called *Household Furniture* by George Smith, published in London in 1808. It contains detailed drawings of buttoned and tufted chairs and couches that are relatively low to the ground and deep, giving a cozy and sheltered feeling to the sitter. These very pieces have been manufactured continuously ever since. An English company calling itself "George Smith" opened in the United States in the late 1980s, returning these styles to popularity. Other manufacturers have jumped on

Right:
HARRY
Galactica sofa
17 yards

the bandwagon and are producing George Smith–inspired furniture in all price ranges.

This style of furniture is often upholstered in soft-colored, faded-looking linens designed or influenced by the English firm of Bennison or in heavy material that looks like Turkish flat-weave *kilim* rugs. However, virtually any fabric from tapestry to chintz can be used on these pieces.

DREXEL
HERITAGE

*9100 series
sectional*

36 yards

Other Victorian sofas had wooden frames, often ornately carved. Some had Gothic or Italianate decorative detailing—this was the age of individuality. Many interesting pieces have been reproduced from originals in historic houses in this country and England. For high-style pieces, tapestry, plush or velvet would be the upholstery fabric of choice. Less formal furniture may be covered in any traditional fabric.

Another Victorian innovation was to place two sofas at a right angle in a corner, anticipating the modern sectional sofa. Victorians considered themselves the culmination of history and embraced all the styles of the past enthusiastically, with the result that today's antiques shops are filled with Neo-Gothic, Neo-classical, Neo-French and Neo-Renaissance furniture, all avidly pursued by collectors.

Art Deco and Atomic

Though much admired, extreme modernist furniture is too demanding for most homes. Other, softer styles have always been popular simultaneously. Many people today prize a chic Parisian style from the 1920s called Art Deco, a comfortable, luxurious style much influenced by jazz. Sofa shapes are simple but fabrics are combined in a special way, with the arms often in a different material from the back and seat. This furniture, incidentally, was even in its early days often sold in department stores rather than commissioned by particular patrons as in the past.

Genuine Art Deco couches are becoming ever more scarce and expensive as collectors scour the market. This fact has not escaped furniture manufacturers, so Deco-inspired furniture is coming on to the market regularly. The designs of Eileen Gray, an Englishwoman who worked in Paris in

DONGHIA

Main Street club sofa

14 yards

SHARPE
NICHOLS

*Paris club
sofa*

14 yards

IKEA

*910404
Karlsboro
sofa*

12 yards

the 1920s and '30s, are being reproduced by several manufacturers; the Deco influence is so strong now that Jay Spectre's collection of Eileen Gray reinterpretations is reputed to be the best-selling designer line in furniture history.

Deco has some similarities with Biedermeier furniture. Light-colored woods were often used —but by the 1920s the frame was often molded plywood. Upholstery shapes were rounded and sensuous. Many of the original fabrics are still

RJONES
Capital sofa

11 yards

furniture. Light-colored woods were often used —but by the 1920s the frame was often molded plywood. Upholstery shapes were rounded and sensuous. Many of the original fabrics are still available. They were strongly influenced by exciting developments in the art of the period such as the faceted shapes of Cubism and the garish purples, oranges and greens of Ballet Russe sets and costumes. At the other extreme, rooms painted and upholstered entirely in white were a hallmark of the period. Exotic natural materials such as leopard pelts and sharkskin were all the rage. Printed materials in these patterns are available today and are most appropriate for this furniture.

In the 1940s the enforced emigrations of World War II moved the center of furniture design to America, where designers like Eero Saarinen and Charles and Ray Eames reinterpreted earlier icons for a wider public and experimented with new materials like plastic and foam rubber. In Scandinavia, too, well-designed and inexpensive furniture was made available to middle-class homes. Most of the wood-framed, often collapsible, Danish sofas of this era have

CENTURY

*16-941
Jay Spectre
steamer sofa*

10.5 yards

THAYER
COGGIN

*436-201
Fire & Ice
sectional*

42 yards

HARRY
*Atomic
Delite sofa*
16 yards

In the '50s, plywood and chrome were still used for frames; plastic imitation leather was a favorite upholstery material. Real leather or fabric in an "atomic" (planets and space ships) or tropical print might be more pleasant to live with.

CHAPTER 3

The Inside Story

No matter what style a couch may be, what most people really want from the furniture is comfort for the many hours spent sitting or lying on it. It's worth taking a little time in the beginning to make sure it feels as good as it looks. A couch should also last as long as possible in good shape. Assuring this involves learning a few basics about how couches are built.

What's inside any couch is a kind of mystery. You can't see it and, at least at first, you can't feel it, but it has a lot to do with how comfortable the furniture is and how long it will last. The structure of a couch is simple: it's a *frame*, usually wooden, supporting a seating structure consisting of *springs* or *foam* pads. *Padding*—some soft material such as fiberfill or down—is wrapped around the structural elements for comfort. *Cushions* may be attached or simply laid on the seat and/or back.

Much of the cost of the couch depends on the quality of these few components. Any couch will be reasonably comfortable at first, but over the years badly constructed frames will wobble and cheap padding will get lumpy. So, for a piece of furniture you plan to keep, the investment in solid construction pays off. On the other hand a temporary piece—for a rented first apartment, for instance—should be as inexpensive a couch as possible.

Couch structure is made up of several components, each of which plays a role in the comfort and durability of the piece of furniture.

❀❀ THE FRAME ❀❀

Most couches are wood-framed. In a few special cases, frames may be metal; some couches are frameless, held together by slats pushed through pockets in the upholstery material. These are unlikely to prove very long-lasting. Always ask what wood the frame is made of and how it is held together. If at all possible, the frame should be of hardwood, such as maple or hickory, that has been kiln-dried. It should be held together with wooden dowels and metal screws. Nowadays, staples and nails, which are less

Double-doweled joints and corner blocks glued and screwed into the frame to maintain rigidity and prevent twisting and wobbling.

Legs engineered into the frame for strength and stability. Hand rubbed finish on all wood parts.

Durable 5/4" and 6/4" kiln-dried hardwood frames that offer strength and resist warping and cracking.

Four rows of double coils, 8-way hand-tied to stay in position.

Coated steel-mesh base to provide solid support and less stress on springs and cushions; insulated to prevent squeaking.

Numerous layers of foam and fiber for contoured comfort.

Inner-spring seat cushions wrapped in polyester or fiber and sewn individually encased in ticking.

Century Furniture Company

desirable, are often used to hold the frame together. Softwood frames, made of pine or spruce, are far less sturdy than hardwood and are virtually always stapled. A softwood frame is acceptable only in a couch intended for short-term use.

Information about the frame should be included on the label, but to see for yourself, lift the couch. This is the first test of structural strength. Hardwood is much heavier than soft-

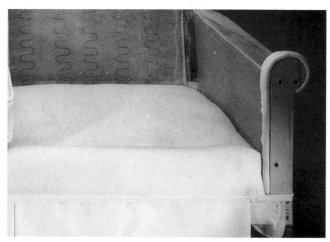

The shape of the frame underlies the padding and sets the style of the couch.

wood. Look under the skirt or, better yet, turn the couch over so you can see the bottom. Don't assume that the legs you see are the same wood as the frame unless they are actually part of the frame, as they should be. Screwed-on legs are a giveaway of poor construction. Push and twist the back and arms—they should not move. This is the second important test.

The shape of the couch should be established by the frame. Curves (including the camelback) or sculptural effects that are supported only by filling will soon collapse. Any exposed wooden parts of the frame should be smooth and well finished.

The depth and *pitch* of the frame (the angle of seat to back) are most important for comfort. The depth should fit the size of the user: if most of the people who will be using the sofa regularly are less than average height, they will probably not be comfortable in a very deep-seated couch; tall people, on the other hand, need more room for their long legs. The pitch, too, might be determined by height—short people will struggle to escape from a deeply back-slanted seat—but also by the use to which the couch will be put. The seat of a couch for reading and watching TV might lean back more than one in a living room used primarily for formal occasions. Two people of extremely different heights who wish to share a sofa will need to learn the art of compromise.

Since you can't see how the frame is held together, you'll have to ask. The salesperson may claim that stapling is just as good as doweling, but every upholsterer interviewed disagrees. If a good frame after some years' use loosens up, it's easy to knock it apart and fit new dowels in place. The metal screws holding the joints together can be reseated. If a nail or staple works its way loose, it may be impossible to fit the frame back together. Insist, if you can, on dowels and screws.

With this basic knowledge, it should be possible to locate a well-framed couch in any price range, since the frame accounts for only a small fraction of the cost.

❧❧ INNER STRUCTURE ❧❧

In fully upholstered couches, the seat, back and arms are usually supported by woven strips of jute (the natural fiber used to make rope) or synthetic webbing. Tied on to the webbing are steel springs, which should be as close together as possible for even support. The best construction is called *eight-way hand-tied coiled spring*. This simply means that each spring, made of special steel wire, is attached by knotted twine to the eight surrounding springs. This process must be done by hand and assures that the springs move independently but interact smoothly. In less expensive constructions, fewer springs are tied together fewer ways—typically six ways. This makes for uneven support as the gaps between the springs are wider. Eventually the twine is likely to break under the strain of trying to hold the seat together.

One alternative form of springing is called *no-sag* or *zigzag*. The springs, which are flat and run horizontally, are attached to the frame itself rather than being held in place by webbing. Another is *Flex-o-lator*, a flat grid of steel that is commonly attached to the frame by springs. It gives the firmest support. Many modern sofa seats with a hard-edged look consist of zigzag springs or a steel grid supporting a dense foam pad. Any of the three types of springs may support the back of the couch, depending on the furniture style.

Test the coiled spring structure by removing

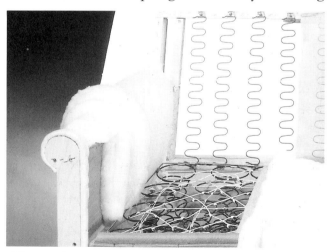

Zigzag springs often support the back of a couch; stronger eight-way hand-tied springs are beneath the seat.

couch seat cushions, revealing the *deck* (which may be covered in a plainer fabric than the rest of the upholstery). Push down to feel how close together and how substantial the springs are. They should give, but neither squeak nor collapse under pressure. If you can feel the coiled wire clearly, the padding is too thin. Push against the back to be sure the support is even. In foam construction, feel through the bottom of the seat to make sure zigzag springs are close together and evenly spaced.

The *foam pad*, whether used in conjunction with springs or set on a wooden platform, should be of high enough density to keep its resilience for a long time. Manufacturers often save money by using low-quality foam. If the maker of the couch provides specifications for the piece, look for a minimum foam density of 1.8 pounds per cubic foot, according to John Hutton, design director of Donghia Furniture/Textiles. Anything lighter is suitable only for padding, not support.

Hand-tied spring construction is often much more expensive than foam, but it lasts longer and many people find it more comfortable. Springs lend themselves to the softer curves of traditional furniture, whereas foam is specified for the clean lines of much modern design. Construction is therefore often ruled by style.

❧❧ FILLING AND PADDING ❧❧

The springs and frame are too hard to sit on directly, so they're covered with soft materials. *Polyurethane foam* in a lighter density than that used for support is one common padding, especially for the back and arms of the couch. *Polyester fiberfill* is another choice, widely used instead of the cotton *batting* and *horsehair* that were once universally found in fine furniture. The top layer of filling may be made of *fiberfill, feathers and down* or pure *down* (underfeathers of fowl, usually geese, making the softest possible stuffing—and the most expensive). This soft filling is often encased between two layers of material that are chambered or quilted, holding it in place without lumps. Some custom upholsterers still insist on horsehair and down, but many of the finest furniture builders maintain that the modern stuffings are as good if not better than the old. The filling content should be on the label. If not, ask.

A very traditional way of anchoring the filling and adding support to the furniture is *tufting* and *buttoning*. A number of stitches are taken at intervals from bottom to top of the seat or back of the couch (through the filling), anchored with a button and pulled tightly back to the bottom. This compresses the filling, providing firm support as well as a decorative pattern. The stitches may also be finished with tufts or tassels in matching or contrasting fabrics.

When considering a buttoned couch, be sure that the buttons are evenly spaced and firmly attached through the stuffing. If both the seat and back are tufted with no cushions to provide extra comfort, poke the stuffing extra carefully to be sure there are no potential problem areas.

Whatever the style, feel all around a couch as you look it over. The padding should be even, with no lumps; the metal springs or the wood frame should not protrude near the surface. Insufficiently padded hard materials will soon wear through the sofa covering.

❧ CUSHIONS ❧

Most couches have cushions on the seat and, often, on the back for comfort and support. Cushion filling is similar to that of the couch itself. Most frequently the support comes from dense foam, either on its own or wrapped in softer foam or polyester batting. Seat cushions, which are firmer than those in back, may contain springs wrapped in cotton, fiberfill, feathers or down. All sorts of combinations of materials are involved in making a comfortable couch.

All these cushion fillings are good—the choice should be made on the basis of what you find most comfortable. Good quality foam cushions give strong support and always look immaculate. Springs will probably outlast foam, but foam is easy and cheap to replace. Feathers and down are softer than fiberfill but less resilient.

Cushions containing down, even in combination with springs, will need fluffing to keep them looking neat. Many decorators—especially the fanciest ones—insist on all-down cushions on the

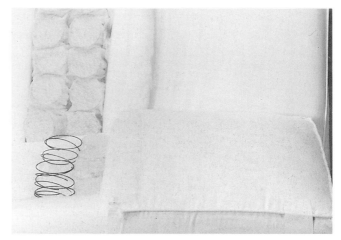

Soft materials add comfort to a sprung seat.

custom couches they specify for their clients. Sitting on these is like sitting on a cloud—the sitter sinks right through to the bottom of the seat. Although this sort of cushion is by far the most expensive and has the reputation of being the most luxurious, many people, in fact, do not like the unsupported feeling. And all-down cushions need fluffing every time they are sat on or they look as messy as an unmade bed. The combina-

Frames and cushions should be guaranteed for the lifetime of the original purchaser.

Flow matching of fabric so that patterns appear to flow uninterrupted through the piece.

Well-padded back and sides for a more luxurious feel and appearance and to provide greater durability.

Loose pillows individually encased.

Well-padded arms, backs, and seats for comfort, shape and long life.

CENTURY
66-309 sofa
19 yards

tion of springs and down may be much more comfortable and quite luxurious enough.

Some cushions are attached to the couch frame, which keeps them in place at all times. Most, however, are loose and can be moved around to equalize wear and soiling. The cushions of a couch are usually square, rectangular or T-shaped. The "T" is the part in front of a set-back arm. Cushion covers normally have zippers that are used only in the manufacturing process— if the filling is removed, the pillow may never return to its original shape. Both sides of the cushions should be equally well finished so they look right when turned. The filling should be evenly distributed with no lumps or empty corners, and all of the cushions should fit the couch neatly with no gaps.

Luxurious cushions containing down can add a lot to the cost of a couch. On the other hand, it's the cushions that make the couch feel more or less comfortable and comfort is a completely personal matter. Before making a final choice, sit, wiggle and lie down on all sorts of cushions. You may find that you really prefer the resilience of foam. Or it may be clear that paying extra for down will return dividends in comfort for the life of the couch.

WHY HAVE A COUCH CUSTOM-MADE?

A lot of decorators (like some quoted in "Tricks of the Trade," p. 137) feel deeply that a couch *must* be custom-made to get the highest quality. And they will maintain that a custom piece is no more expensive than a good ready-made sofa.

It is true that at the high end of the market a ready-made couch may cost nearly as much as custom—though the all-down specials so many decorators love cost more than any couch in a store. And if you must have all-down, it will need to be custom-made. Dealing with a custom workroom, the exact size, height and shape are specified. Which is a great advantage *as long as you know exactly what you want.*

The fact is that few people are expert enough at visualizing furniture to identify just those details that will make the couch perfect. So, in practice, the decorator or upholsterer makes the decisions and hopes you like the result. If not, you can make expensive changes or you can live with it and hope to learn to love it.

Stanley Hura is a decorator and designer who has created a lot of custom couches for clients, but has also designed several retail upholstery collections for the Pearson Company, a nationally distributed manufacturer. He says he uses ready-made couches whenever possible. He admires "the many wonderful pieces that are readily available across the board from Pearson and other fine companies" and does not feel it's necessary to have a couch custom-made to get good quality. He suggests that consumers do their homework both in stores and in magazines, then "sit in the furniture—don't just order from a catalog" because comfort is important. After identifying a comfortable couch, choose upholstery and detailing from the manufacturer's catalog. "So many retail companies do custom work—they will give you any filling along with the custom details you want" and the price is usually much less than for true custom work.

Most people are simply more comfortable buying a big and expensive piece of furniture like a couch after sitting on it in a store. Nowadays the manufacturers offer many options of length, filling and pillows—to say nothing of fabric, arm and skirt design, and trimming, which will be covered in the next chapters. The lines between retail and custom are blurring, to the great advantage of the consumer.

THE INSTANT GUEST ROOM

To use living space regularly for sleeping, it is best to buy a sofa that converts to a bed. An ordinary couch is not built heavily enough for constant use as a sleeper.

Convertible, fold-out sofas contain mattresses that are quite comfortable, though not quite as heavily constructed as standard mattresses. They are supported on zigzag springs and wire, which are less durable than the box springs sold for bedding but entirely strong enough for occasional use. A convertible sofa is nearly indistinguishable in style from an ordinary couch, except for the back, which is deeper to accommodate the folded mattress. It is important to take this into account, as well as the space needed to extend the bed, when measuring the room prior to shopping for a couch.

The backs of some convertible sofas drop to the same level as the seat to form a mattress. This reduces the measurements of the closed couch and can make a fairly comfortable bed if the couch is substantially constructed. The sleeper's comfort is much improved by putting a thick pad under the bottom sheet.

LA-Z-BOY

51-663 Cumberland queen sleep sofa

17 yards

IKEA

Prinsessan sleep sofa

13 yards

IKEA

*Marienbad
sleep sofa*

13 yards

NOT FOR NAPS ONLY

I.L.EURO

Cappellini Jasper Morrison daybed

8 yards

GRANGE

Consulate convertable sofa bed

12 yards

Daybeds are actually single beds with headboards and footboards and sometimes a rail on one of the long sides, placed lengthwise against a wall or in an alcove. Since even a single bed mattress is wider than a couch seat, daybeds are usually thickly piled with cushions and pillows to make them comfortable for sitting. Daybeds often have wooden exterior frames, their deep sides hiding the box spring that supports the upholstered mattress. Western-style couches (often referred to as "Taos" furniture) and the popular French-inspired sleigh beds are often used as daybeds. Though once considered appropriate only for after-lunch naps, a daybed may be the only bed in a modern studio apartment.

FOLDABLE FUTONS

A futon on a frame is still the sofa/bed combination chosen by many young people. Futons are a translation from the space-savvy Japanese, who have for generations slept on firm mattresses that can be folded up and put away during the day.

Fillings available include long-staple cotton, feathers or a combination of foam and one of the other fillings.

The mattress is covered with a tightly woven cotton fabric and rests on a folding hardwood frame that converts easily from upright to horizontal. Futon covers in a variety of upholstery fabrics and sheetings are available to change the furniture from day to night use. Any of these sofa bed choices can double the use of a living room or den at extremely moderate cost, which explains their popularity.

AMERICAN
FUTON

Futon Sofa

THE FLEXIBLE SECTIONAL

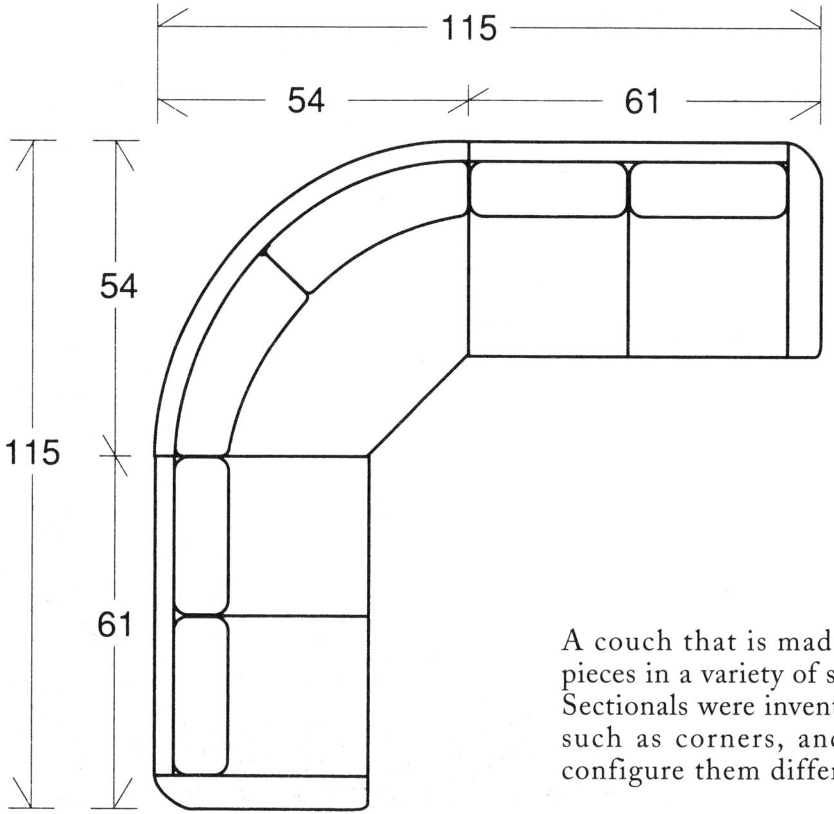

115

54   61

54

115

61

A couch that is made up of several matching pieces in a variety of shapes is called a sectional. Sectionals were invented to fill awkward spaces, such as corners, and to allow the owner to configure them differently in different rooms.

Swaim

DOMUS

Lobby sectional

35 yards

Although sectionals are often used in offices, they are also suitable for family rooms and living rooms, especially for people who move house often. As the owner's needs change, good sectional pieces can be used on their own or combined into two or more separate pieces of furniture. They come in every style from the most traditional to ultra-modern. Typical "sections" include: right and left end pieces, armless chairs, square or curved corners, sofa beds, one-armed chaises longues.

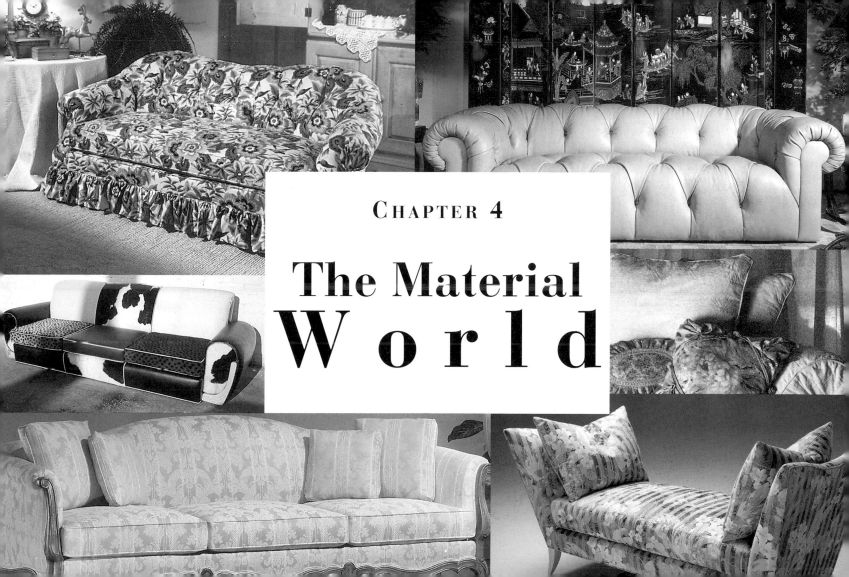

CHAPTER 4

The Material
World

Choosing upholstery fabric is the second major decision (after style) when buying a couch, and it's the most important to the look of the piece. In sofas, as so often in life, the surface counts more at first than what's inside—and the first impression of a couch, no matter what the style or construction, comes from the fabric covering it. Changing the fabric can make the same couch look remarkably different; the real expression of individual taste comes in the choice of upholstery. Will the room be formal or relaxed? Country-simple or sophisticated? The choice of a formal floral over a soft, nubby tweed will communicate the style, so it is important to spend time thinking about the atmosphere of the finished room when selecting a fabric.

The other major consideration in choosing fabric is, as always, cost. Selecting a multicolored print on linen rather than on a plain cotton blend can shoot the price of a large couch into the budget–breaking category—especially if it is a large pattern that needs matching. This is why it's important to make style and structure choices first. Keep in mind one of the cardinal rules of successful couch-buying: INVEST IN THE BEST-PROPORTIONED AND -CONSTRUCTED COUCH YOU CAN POSSIBLY AFFORD. CHANGE THE FABRIC LATER. It is perfectly possible to order a good-quality sofa in an inexpensive plain material or even in muslin (the coarse fabric covering applied by the manufacturer—it is normally covered by upholstery in a better material) with an informal slipcover. Everyone will think you're wisely protecting the elegant fabric underneath. A good couch will be in mint condition structurally for several years, so later, when the budget has recovered, the couch can be reupholstered in a more impressive fabric.

COUTURE FOR COUCHES

Upholstery is the equivalent of a designer dress or tailor-made suit. It should look and feel as good for years as when it's new—which will happen only if it's made of good fabric, properly cut and fitted to the frame and filling of the couch. And since even an inexpensive couch costs as much as designer clothing and will last much longer, it should be as well made and finished as the budget allows.

A slipcover can change the look of a couch completely.

LEE
3099SL
sofa
17 yards

Before beginning the process of choosing fabric, it is essential to make sure that the furniture manufacturer builds his product with care. Is the fabric firmly and smoothly attached to the frame? No lumps, bumps or loose places are acceptable at any price. Check edges, buttons, tufts, hems—all of the finishing details should be neatly sewn and solidly attached.

As is apparent from looking at magazines and shopping the stores, there are literally thousands of fabrics out there. Between fabric stores and the various designer sources, options proliferate. The challenge is to choose the one that's right for both the couch and the room.

The place to begin the search is with the fabrics the manufacturer has chosen for each specific couch. The store will have samples of these materials grouped by price; the manufacturer keeps them all in stock and can deliver the couch covered in any of them quite quickly. If the price difference is important, it is wise to limit oneself to affordable groups—otherwise the most expensive material will surely seem the most attractive.

Even within limits, there will be a dizzying number of swatches to choose from. Finding an acceptable material from the manufacturer's stock will save time and energy.

Having narrowed the choice to one or two likely candidates, ask the salesperson for a *memo sample* (usually a half-yard or so) or a *swatch* to look at in the light of the room where it will be used. Colors vary with light; what looks like peach in the store may be orange at home. If the final decision is close, it's worth paying for memo samples if necessary. Often the cost will be deducted from the final purchase price.

If none of the manufacturer's samples is quite right, ask if other choices are available. Sometimes the store has other materials in stock. If not, the manufacturer will usually accept fabric bought from another source. In furniture jargon, this is called *COM* (Customer's Own Material). There is often an additional charge for this privilege—another reason to accept one of the manufacturer's selections. Custom and to-the-trade furniture is always covered temporarily in muslin and upholstered *COM*. When the couch is ordered, the manufacturer or custom upholsterer will specify the required yardage. The fabric supplier will deliver it either to you or to the store or upholsterer.

Upholstery fabrics come in several widths, from European weaves as narrow as 36 inches to certain kinds of sailcloth and theatrical linen that may be up to 100 inches wide. The vast majority of upholstery materials are between 45 and 60 inches wide, with 54 inches the most common width. Obviously, the width will affect the amount of yardage required and the ultimate price. It may well be, depending on the pattern, that a 54-inch fabric at $25 per yard will end by costing less than a 45-inch material at $20 to cover the same sofa. The store or upholsterer should supply the yardage requirements for several widths.

There are many fabric sources, both retail and to-the-trade, in the back of this book. If a to-the-trade showroom does not allow consumers to buy directly, take the name, stock and color number of the material and either contact a decorator or start calling the telephone discounters listed in this book and in the back of design magazines. With perseverance, virtually any fabric can be located. Retail fabric shops, which usually advertise in local newspapers and yellow pages, are another good resource. In any case, get memo samples or swatches to examine the fabric at home. When shopping in a deep discount place that doesn't cut swatches, examine the fabric in natural light to prevent unpleasant surprises later. Once the yardage is cut, it can't be returned. Remember, while color and pattern are important, it's essential that the upholstery be of the right quality to wear well.

Durability

One reason to collect a group of memos and swatches is to scrutinize them in detail and test their quality. Pulling and scratching at the sample in the store may not be possible, but every fabric should be put to the test before buying. Besides looking good, the couch must hold up for years of use.

Tightly woven fabrics (with many threads per inch) generally wear best. They hold their shape and stretch very little. When a tightly woven fabric is held up to the light, no light should shine through. Hold each swatch by the edges and pull hard. The fabric should not give or slip at all. Then hold the swatch by opposite corners and pull (this is called *on the bias*). It will give somewhat, but even with a hard tug should not feel as though it's coming apart. If the fabric is scratched with a fingernail, there should not be any long threads that can be loosened easily by catching on clothing or by children or pets playing on the furniture—which can happen even in the best-regulated households.

If the ideal material is a less-substantial fabric, don't despair. There are two ways to strengthen a loosely woven or lightweight fabric. One is *quilting:* stitching the lighter material (usually cotton or linen) in an allover pattern to a stronger fabric with a soft filling sandwiched between the layers. Or, less expensive fabrics may be *backed* with latex for strength, but beware. Heavy backing usually signals that the material is too loosely woven to hold up for long, even with reinforcement. Accept only a light backing if any; fold the sample in half and rub the backed sides together to be sure it won't flake off. Although quilted and backed materials are fairly sturdy, neither of these solutions will wear as well as a fabric that is tightly woven.

The *fiber content* of fabric is listed on the label. The majority of upholstery materials are blends teaming natural fibers like cotton or wool with synthetics, such as nylon and olefin, which add durability. Many of the most expensive fabrics are woven of pure natural fibers. They are often very beautiful but generally don't wear as well as the blends. Silk, the most expensive of fibers, is particularly delicate and recommended only for upholstery that will be lightly used. On the other hand, pure synthetics rarely feel as luxurious as naturals—hence the popularity of blends.

The last—and very important—aspect of

fabric durability is how often and how well it can be cleaned. Obviously light colors show soil sooner than dark; plain colors sooner than patterns; smooth surfaces sooner than textured. Synthetics resist soiling but, once soiled, natural fibers clean up better. Many fabrics are coated with soil repellents such as 3M-Scotchgard or DuPont Teflon, including most of those offered by the large upholstered-furniture manufacturers. Sometimes coating is available for an extra charge from either the furniture manufacturer or the fabric showroom. If the couch has been made in uncoated fabric (a floor sample, for instance) there are several companies that spray coating on furniture. The store may recommend one, or they may be listed in the yellow pages. As a painstaking last resort, housewares stores sell spray cans of coating to be applied at home. A couch that will take heavy wear should have some soil-resistant coating.

Once the furniture starts getting soiled, it must be cleaned before the dirt gets too deeply embedded. Minor spots may be removed with one of the widely available spray upholstery cleaners, but major work should be done by a professional specialist. Vacuuming the fabric regularly and rotating loose cushions will even out the soiling and wear. The cushion covers, however, should never be removed for cleaning. It is extremely difficult to replace the filling properly.

Among the most durable fabrics for upholstery are:

tapestry weave

twill

velvet

matelassé

frieze

union cloth (cotton and linen blend)

ruglike (kilim) weaves

LEATHER FOR UPHOLSTERY

Leather is the most expensive material for upholstery and, some people think, the best. In less expensive couches, leather-look vinyl is sometimes substituted for the real thing. Suede and suede-like synthetics are also popular for top-of-the-line upholstery. Here's the lowdown on these premium materials:

Which leathers are the best for upholstery?

Good quality upholstery leather is dyed right through the skin and is nearly as supple as fabric. Stiff leather does not fit smoothly around the curves of a couch and will crack with wear. Of course, leather, which is chosen partly for its great durability, should be fairly substantial. Glove leather, which is very thin and soft, is beautiful but will not hold up to wear.

The very best vinyls should have the same characteristics as leathers and may be satisfactory for upholstery as long as the finish is not too shiny.

What about suede?

Fine suede, a soft-surfaced leather, is durable for upholstery but shows wear and soiling. A better choice is one of the imitations that are practically indistinguishable from genuine suede, wear well and are very easy to clean with soap and water.

Can you clean leather?

Leather is the most durable covering you can put on a couch, and true lovers of leather appreciate the signs of wear that will inevitably appear over the years. Even cat scratches are less damaging to leather than to fabric.

Leather will darken on the arms as oils from people's skin sinks in, but again this is considered part of the charm of a well-used sofa. Regular saddle-soaping will slow soiling while keeping the leather supple. For the fewest possible changes as the couch wears, it can be covered in distressed leather, which from the start shows variations in texture and color.

What does it cost?

As with fabric, the cost of leather varies with the quality. However, it generally costs between 50 percent more and double the price for the best leather and suede as compared with the best fabric. Vinyl is cheaper than leather; ersatz suede costs about the same as the genuine article—the savings come with easier upkeep.

Which styles are the best for leather couches?

The classic leather sofa style is the tufted chesterfield so long associated with men's clubs and bachelor pads. It is still extremely popular for its comfort, durability and great style. Tailored styles in general are best for leather. Plain backs and seats are better than loose cushions. If the couch has cushions, be sure they have vents in the back and don't make a rude noise when sat on. Leather and suede are thicker than fabric, so arms with few pleats will look better than elaborately gathered ones. A leather couch should sit on plain or bun feet—no skirts or ruffles.

PALAZZETTI

Dynamic sofa by David Shaw Nichols

10 yards

LEXINGTON

*8321-33
Timberlake
leather
camelback
sofa*

18 yards

HaRry

Club easy sofa

18 yards

LEE
INDUSTRIES
3094 sofa
14.5 yards

Color

Before selecting a color for the couch, present living arrangements should be taken into account. When decorating a home for many years of use, the upholstery should be tied into the overall color scheme and other fabric choices. If, on the other hand, the couch will probably be moved to other surroundings in a year or so, it is wiser to choose a neutral that will look good anywhere. This principle explains the large number of beige couches in the world.

Even for a temporary dwelling, consider using a color more practical and individual than beige (unless beige is your favorite color). Perhaps there's a basic color—green, burgundy or

THAYER COGGIN

200-203 City Lights Collection sofa

15 yards

🧹🧹🧹

dark blue, for example—that can function as a neutral. After the move, a new decorating scheme can be built around the same favorite color.

When planning the decoration of a room, some people start with the wall color, others with fabric and still others with some precious object such as a painting or Oriental rug. Whatever the starting point, the couch is usually covered in a fairly unobtrusive fabric that blends with the sur-

roundings. A sofa in an assertive color and/or pattern will dominate most rooms by sheer size. In a very large room, or when the couch needs to stand out, shocking pink or huge bouquets may be the right choice. In decades past, curtains and couches were often made in the same material. This looks a little too studied for today's eclectic decorating style.

Narrow the color choices as much as possible. It may be desirable to pick up either the peach or the green in the floral chintz chosen for curtains; perhaps it's the red or the blue in the kilim rug. An effective room may feature a modern pale color scheme or a rich, traditional one inspired by an English gentleman's library. Decorators make a "board" for each room to show clients how the elements work together. It's often helpful to imitate the pros, pasting or stapling each paint chip and fabric swatch on a piece of poster board. As elements are added the picture will take shape.

HARDEN
6078 sofa
19 yards

Whatever color is selected, the yardage must all be cut from the same bolt. As fabric is woven and printed over time, the colors are remixed when one batch runs out. In theory, the same formula is always used; in practice, variations always occur. At a retail store, have the fabric measured out and cut as you watch. When ordering fabric from a trade showroom or a telephone discounter, specify that all yardage be from the same dye lot and if possible be in one piece. If the

THOMASVILLE
283-9 sofa
18.5 yards

fabric is to be delivered to you as opposed to the upholsterer or store, check to be sure that the pieces match your sample and each other. Variation from the sample may be so minor that the fabric is perfectly acceptable; however, two or more unmatched pieces should be rejected as the variations will show in the finished upholstery.

THOMASVILLE
854-7
16 yards

Once the family of colors for the couch has been chosen, the question of pattern arises. Choices include plain colors, tweeds, stripes, plaids, florals, flamestitches, Art Deco tapestries, to name just a few. There is a lot to look at.

It may seem simplest to select a plain fabric, but it soon becomes apparent that solid colors come in many textures. Smooth, flat finishes in plain colors show wear soonest of all fabrics and in general are not suitable for upholstery. For the quietest effect, an unobtrusive woven texture, such as *twill* (a diagonally ribbed weave), *velvet* (a smooth cut pile), *frieze* (uncut pile loops), or *dobby* (a small regular pattern in the weave that is visible only from close up), is a good choice.

Other fabrics gain decorative punch from the weave. Repp has distinct ribs running with the grain; damask contrasts satin and dull surfaces in a repeated design; *matelassé* is a double weave that looks something like quilting. To create a strong pattern, repp is dampened and heat-treated to produce *moiré* alternating areas of cut and uncut loops make *figured* or *cut velvet*. *Chenille* is another popular fabric woven of fuzzy yarn that gives it a most appealing softness. The visual richness of these weaves adds interest to solid colors.

Somewhere between a plain and a pattern is *tweed*, where yarns of several colors are twisted together and woven as one. Tweed is slow to show soiling because of the mix of colors.

Patterns using more than one color are either *woven* or *printed*—the difference can be seen on

SHELTON MINDEL & ASSOC. FOR JACK LENOR LARSEN

Arboretum Collection, Tamarack sofa

17 yards

THOMASVILLE
890-7 sofa
17 yards

the back. A woven stripe, for instance, will be the same on back and front, while the back of a printed stripe will usually be plain. Two- or three-colored *reversible* wovens may have one color dominant on the first side, another on the other. The colored threads that make up the design are carried across the back of one-sided wovens such as *brocades*. The back of a print will either show no pattern or will have uneven color patches where the dye has soaked through.

Plain fabrics and those with allover small patterns are easy to piece together because they can meet anywhere in the yardage. They are the most economical upholstery fabrics, since none of the yardage is wasted in matching. Inexpensive couches will look best in this sort of fabric, since the manufacturers cannot afford wastage at these price levels.

Patterns like *paisleys* with swirling lines are another practical choice for upholstery. The effect is similar to an allover pattern. Not only do they not need matching, the intricacy of the design disguises wear and soiling. As with any fabric,

medium to dark colors will look fresh longer than pales.

Larger-scale patterns are printed on a number of fabrics, such as *chintz*, a plain-surfaced cotton that is usually glazed, linen and damask. *Tapestry* is a woven fabric incorporating intricate multicolored designs, which may be very large in scale. Tapestries were originally worked by hand like modern needlepoint, but now are woven on looms. Designs can be floral, geometric (like the popular *kilim* rug patterns) or abstract.

Most patterned fabrics should be *matched* to look their best. That is: the same part of the pattern should meet at each join so the lines of the pattern are not broken. To achieve this, the fabric must be cut very precisely according to the printed or woven design, which takes extra labor and may result in wastage. The difficulty of matching and the amount of wastage depends on the size of the *repeat*—the distance from the center of one full design to the next. A loose pattern of scattered roses may have a 6-inch repeat, while a stately print of formal bouquets and ribbons may occupy as much as 24 inches. The bigger the repeat, the more material will be wasted to assure that the design is correctly positioned on all surfaces. Take the exact measurements of the couch to a professional to find out how many yards will actually be needed before choosing such a fabric—and be prepared to pay more for both fabric and labor if the match is complicated.

Stripes are the simplest of patterns to match, but the way they are arranged has a very strong effect on the appearance of the couch. Stripes running in the usual vertical way make a couch look taller and slimmer. A couch with the stripes running horizontally (this is called *railroading*) will seem wider. Whichever way they run stripes should ideally be matched at each meeting. Unmatched very narrow stripes in closely related colors (pale blue and white ticking, for example) may be acceptable on extremely inexpensive furniture, but unmatched stripes in strongly

HICKORY
CHAIR

*5052-71
Mark
Hampton
Collection
bamboo sofa*

10.5 yards

THOMASVILLE

*A906-598
sofa*

16.5 yards

HARDEN
*934 love
seat*

8 yards

contrasting colors make a couch look misshapen. *Flamestitch* fabrics (a kind of tapestry with a regular repeating zigzag design) are matched like stripes.

Checks and *plaids* are deceptively simple geometric patterns; matching them is difficult because they must meet precisely both vertically and horizontally. All those straight lines call attention immediately to any short comings in joining. Do not choose them for upholstery unless you are sure of the upholsterer's skills or will not be annoyed by mismatching.

THOMASVILLE
880-8 sofa
14.5 yards

Floral designs, especially bouquets, should be *centered* on the inside and outside surfaces of the back and arms, the cushions and loose pillows if any. This is essential to an elegant couch.

Ideally, the design should also be matched at the meetings of cushions, sofa base and skirt. Perfect matches can waste a lot of material, so only the most expensive couches have them. Often, centering is used instead of perfect matching. For instance, in upholstery using big geometrics like the kilim rug designs now in fashion, the main pattern is centered but the smaller areas are not matched.

Many people find unmatched fabric on a couch a constant annoyance; others hardly notice. To find out how your own eye deals with matching, look closely at the couches in the various stores you visit and in magazine photos. Imagine living with them. If the sight of an unmatched floral makes you jump each time you see it, choose a simpler fabric or be prepared to pay for a good match. If not, you can be more relaxed. But even if the match need not be perfect, large patterns must be centered on the back and cushions or the sofa will look cheap.

LEE INDUSTRIES
3277 sofa
19.5 yards

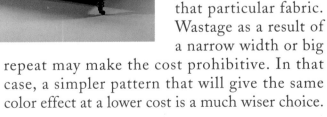

Pictorial designs, whether floral, architectural or otherwise, need to be centered as discussed earlier and matched as completely as possible. It choosing one of these designs, be sure to look at it from a distance. Pictorials can be very assertive and may have a tendency to dominate the decoration. A white background, cheerful as it may look when new, accentuates the contrast and will show soiling and wear sooner than a color, even a pastel. When

ordering any couch, especially a light-colored one, always order extra arm covers in the same fabric. Since the arms show dirt and wear first, this will nearly double the life of the furniture.

All of the above considerations—the width of the fabric, the type of pattern and the size of the repeat—will affect how much material and labor are required to cover a couch. Before committing to a pattern, get accurate information about the exact yardage needed in that particular fabric. Wastage as a result of a narrow width or big repeat may make the cost prohibitive. In that case, a simpler pattern that will give the same color effect at a lower cost is a much wiser choice.

∞∞∞∞∞ *Basic Decorative Choices* ∞∞∞∞∞

At medium to high price levels, most upholstered furniture manufacturers offer choices of arm shapes and skirt detailing on all their couches.

Consult the charts for some of the most popular options, and notice arms and skirts in the stores. Try different arms to see what height and shape is most comfortable as well as attractive. A given couch can be made with a tailored skirt, a soft

SWAIM

889 double chaise

12 yards

one or none at all for a lighter look. Specifying arms and skirts is one of the easiest and least expensive ways to individualize a couch.

Simple trimmings offer another area of choice. *Welting*, the fabric-wrapped cord trim at seams and where fabric meets the wood frame of most couches, may match or contrast with the basic fabric. Contrasting welting accentuates the lines of the couch. *Gimp*, a flat-woven braid, is often used instead of contrasting welting, espe-

Drexel
Heritage
*1007-01
sofa*
9.5 yards

cially around the bottom edge of the seat and on cushions. It is a fairly traditional and formal trim. *Nailheads*, usually in brass, hold the fabric to the frame and provide a traditional decorative accent. In some very formal furniture styles, the nailheads themselves are arranged in patterns such as swags or scallops.

Buttons are another favorite trim for couches. They should be used only with true *tufting*, where a stitch is taken through the entire thickness of the couch from back to front, then pulled through and attached to the frame. The button is normally covered in the upholstery fabric and should be tightly covered and securely anchored. Re-attaching a loose button will require the services of an upholsterer. Sometimes buttons are used purely as trim, stitched only through the front fabric and a layer or two of stuffing. These will invariably come loose sooner or later and are not recommended. True button-and-tuft construction is expensive, and it may be necessary to select another style to keep costs down. The same is true of the dressmaker details—tassels, fringes and elaborate ruffling—discussed further in the next chapter, "Tricks of the Trade." A basic couch should give basic value: money spent on solid construction and good, durable upholstery rather than on fancy trim returns the best dividends.

SKIRTS AND LEGS

Different skirt styles can make a couch look tailored, relaxed or formal. However, it's important to take the fabric into account when specifying the skirt. Stiff wovens look best in more tailored styles, while some of the softer printed cottons will take well to ruffling.

Exposing the legs of a couch can change the style dramatically. Usually the effect is more modern and lighter. For a contemporary look, the legs can be upholstered in the same fabric as the couch.

For decorative detailing to enhance the skirt, see the next chapter, "Tricks of the Trade."

Parson Leg

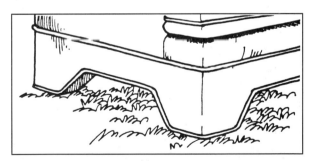

Shell Foot

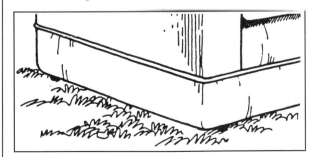

Base to Floor

Skirts and Legs

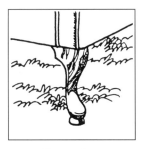

Queen Anne

Chippendale

Ball and Claw

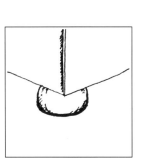

Upholstered

Ungrooved

Grooved

SKIRT STYLES

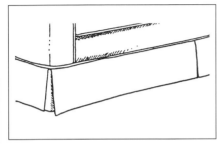

Tuxedo

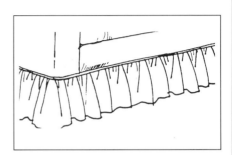

Double Pleated

Ruffled

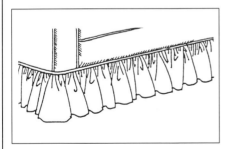

Gathered

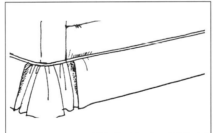

Gathered Insert

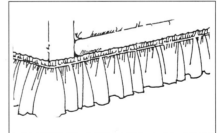

Dressmaker

A CHOICE OF ARMS

Manufacturers offer almost infinite variations in arm detailing. Tops may be round, square or T-shaped, the fabric smoothly stretched, pleated or gathered. Seams and welting may be accented at the edges only or may form a panel in the middle of the arm. Looking at the arms of sofas in magazines and stores, as well as trying them out for comfort, helps in finding the most appropriate style.

Illustrated here are a selection of popular arm options from many manufacturers. Each furniture company has a number of styles from which the final choice can be made.

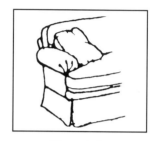

*Pleated Arm
Straight Cushion*

*Pleated Arm
T-Cushion*

*English Arm
T-Cushion*

*Track Arm
Straight Cushion*

*Track Arm
T-Cushion*

Century Furniture Company

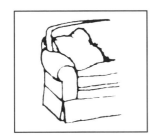

Sock Arm
Straight Cushion

Sock Arm
T Cushion

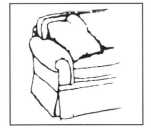

Lawson Arm
Straight Cushion

Lawson Arm
T-Cushion

LA-Z-BOY

51-663
Cumberland
sleep sofa

12 yards

Reupholstering—Worth the Trouble?

Suppose you already have a couch, though it's worn and you're tired of the upholstery. It seems a waste to throw it out and in most places it's not easy to get rid of such a big, cumbersome item. Or, a terrific shape in hideous fabric turns up at a thrift shop. New sofas are expensive, so maybe the old one or the thrift shop bargain can be re-covered. But after seeing an estimate on repair and a new cover from the local upholsterer and finding out the price of 15 to 20 yards of fabric, it becomes clear that reupholstery is an investment, too. It will be worth doing only if:

∽The frame is sound. If the back or arms wiggle or the legs squeak when you sit down, the frame is probably shot. Even a good hardwood frame may need some new pegs or screws, but repairs to a stapled softwood frame will not be worth the money.

∽The springs are in good shape. Some rewebbing and retying can be worthwhile on a good couch, but if the springs have lost their spring, it's time to get a new sofa. If the couch is foam rubber, the foam will probably need to be replaced, which may or may not pay.

∽The stuffing is fairly good. If the couch is an old one with horsehair stuffing, it can be refluffed for more years of use. Fiberfill and down can be added to cushions and backs which have flattened over time.

If the couch was a fine piece of furniture from the beginning, it's probably worth rebuilding. If it's out of style but in fine structural condition, consider slipcovering. If you bought it for a song years ago and your attachment is purely sentimental, start over with a new couch. You'll learn to love it.

YOUR SLIPCOVER IS SHOWING

In fact, your slipcover is *meant* to show. It's the icing on the cake, a magic transformer that lets the couch change identities at will. A red couch can turn blue, a formal love seat jazzy, a somber silk sofa into a cozy chintz conversation piece.

The earliest slipcovers, in the eighteenth and nineteenth centuries, were ordered at the same time and from the same supplier as the upholstered furniture they covered. Their function was pure protection; they could usually be washed and were replaced when worn, at much less cost than reupholstering the piece. They were made in plain materials like linen, cotton or wool, and tightly fitted to look as much like upholstery as possible. Slipcovers were considered good enough for family use but were always removed when honored guests arrived.

It didn't take homeowners long to see that slipcovering afforded a great opportunity for a new look at a low price. The first timid attempts consisted of using striped or checkered linen covers held to the frame by hooks and eyes or bowknots. It's said that Americans were the first to dress up the slipcovers with ruffles and fringes. Skilled upholsterers were scarce in the Colonies, so slipcovers did heavy duty for long periods.

As printed fabrics became more colorful and less expensive, they were widely used for slipcovers. Chintz, in fact, was considered strictly a slipcover material until the late Victorian era, when it began to be used for upholstery. Slipcovering became fashionable; the French, always testing the outer limits of fashion, often had four sets for each piece of furniture—one for each season. Often the upholstery was never actually seen at all!

From the Victorian era until today, furniture styles have tended to change every few years. Nineteenth-century homeowners discovered that slipcovering would let them keep up with the Joneses without throwing out perfectly

serviceable if outmoded furniture. Within reason, this holds true today. Even the cleverest slipcover can't change a tubular-steel foam rubber divan into a deep-buttoned chesterfield, but lesser miracles may quite easily be performed.

A slipcover is the quickest, cheapest way to a decorative facelift. Millions of couches covered in brown velvet or nubby natural cotton sit serviceably in houses and apartments all over America. They're too sturdy to discard but too tired to admire. A slipcover will change the character of one of these boring old couches when it is moved from living room to bedroom or from city apartment to country house. Even if the couch stays in the same spot, covering it in a floral print or richly patterned cotton blend will give it a new lease on life. If the seat and back cushions have flattened with age, add some extra filling before measuring for yardage.

Whether effecting a complete change or simply rejuvenating a favorite couch, there is a slipcover style for every taste and pocketbook, from a simple throw to a ruched and ruffled extravaganza. Slipcovering is simple enough to allow frequent changes as inspiration dictates.

∞∞∞ *Slipcover style* ∞∞∞

Slipcovers may be tight-fitting and plain, imitating upholstery, or they can be loose and ruffled or fringed. Very tight and tailored covers are really only suitable as protection for unusually valuable and delicate upholstery; otherwise a softer, more informal look, usually with skirts to the ground, is preferable. The skirt styles on page 123 can all be adapted for slipcovers.

Some covers are loosely tied on with bows for a very casual look. The quickest and easiest slipcover is simply a length of fabric thrown over the piece of furniture and tucked in around the cushions. Of course, after people have sat on this sort of cover the couch looks literally like an unmade bed.

Whatever the style, covers should be easy to take off and put back on. The whole point is to provide a quick change for the room. Long zippers or velcro strips in accessible places are a great convenience. Some ready-made slipcovers are meant to be anchored with pins, the most efficient of which are plastic-headed spirals available at upholstery supply shops.

Slipcovers, rather than upholstery, are suitable for trying out extreme or ultra-fashionable styles. Each surface might be a different color or pattern. The entire couch can be wrapped in fabric and tied like a gift. Even a fuchsia satin slipcover with rhinestone trim might be created to fulfill a fantasy without breaking the budget, to be succeeded by another, wilder idea.

∞∞∞ *Fabrics for slipcovers* ∞∞∞

Several of the major furniture manufacturers, like their eighteenth-century ancestors, now make slipcovers that can be ordered at the same time as the couch. These are far from the least expensive covers to be found, but since they are made in the original factory they should be a perfect fit. The selection of fabrics is good and ordering this way saves time, if not money. Otherwise local upholsterers, furniture stores and even dressmakers can run up slipcovers. It you're at all handy with a sewing machine you can probably make a simple slipcover yourself. Patterns for slipcovers are sold along with those for dresses.

Any reasonably sturdy material can be used for slipcovers. Common sense dictates that the fabric should be washable, though for a more formal look, one that needs to be dry cleaned might be used. A soil-repellent coating would be welcome in dry-cleanable fabrics, but not in ones which will be tossed into the washing machine.

When choosing slipcover materials, it's important to consider the question of tidiness. The slouchy look is in fashion, but is it for you? Linen, for instance, is one of the most beautiful and traditional slipcover materials. In solid colors (especially natural beige), checks, stripes and florals, it has been used in elegant houses for generations. However, there's one thing to remember about linen: it wrinkles. It's supposed to stretch and get soft-looking, which is considered by linen-lovers to be one of its charms. The sort of person who likes everything neat and smooth will be driven crazy by linen. For sanity's sake, another fabric should be chosen. Natural

canvas piped in green, for instance, will have the elegant country-club look of those Thirties comedies starring Katharine Hepburn, but will take far less upkeep than the linen actually used in the 1930s.

Very attractive slipcovers can be made of plain fabrics. A generation ago in this country the traditional summer covers were those green-piped natural ones and they still look great. Plain white covers can give any furnished rented house an instant facelift. The only problem with solid colors, in slipcovers as well as upholstery, is that they show spots immediately. A pattern woven into the fabric will mitigate this effect somewhat. More practical are checked or striped covers like those seen in old paintings of domestic scenes. These fabrics are still appealing, particularly in an informal country setting.

Chintz, available today in more colors and patterns than ever before, is perfect for slipcovers. If the winter upholstery is somber in color, if the couch is good but dreary, or to transfer that old sofa from the living room to the bedroom,

DREXEL
HERITAGE

*1601 Slip
sofa*

18.5 yards

chintz will make the transformation. On the subject of wrinkles, a heavily glazed chintz made into tightly fitted covers will stay tidy. If, on the other hand, you follow the example of some of the more refined decorators and wash the material to remove the shiny glaze, the weave will become somewhat looser, resulting in some wrinkling. Again, it all depends if wrinkles are acceptable or not in the situation.

To some people, one of the most desirable by-products of washability is fading. They feel that some chintzes, too assertive when new, gain in genteel charm after several washings. Those same, very refined decorators dip new white-background chintzes in a bath of light tea to dull the color and give the room that slightly faded aura of old money. On the other hand, dry cleaning will keep the colors bright.

A decorating trick people have used for centuries is to make slipcovers in the same fabric as curtains or loose cushions. If the upholstery was chosen to blend with the background colors, the room then has two separate coordinated looks. They can be changed seasonally or simply at whim. The slipcovers can be trimmed with piping or braid for a luxurious or frivolous touch. Nonetheless, if the slipcovers are meant to be washable, it would be silly to use a trim that shrinks or is not colorfast.

One of the very best fabrics for slipcovers, which no decorator is likely to suggest, is sheeting. Nowadays, sheets are printed in vibrant colors and sophisticated patterns that, though less than restful for sleeping, are perfect for furniture covers. The enormous area of king-size sheets (108 x 102 inches is typical) means that only two or three of them will cover a couch. The chart on page 136 gives exact yardages for the different sheet sizes.

Sheets are cheap and practically indestructible—those with 50 percent or more synthetic fiber wear like iron. These fabrics are created to keep their color and texture in the washing machine, so are absolutely the most practical choice for covers that will take a lot of use from children and dogs. They're virtually the only sensible choice for pure white summer covers. Beware, though: a dark or strong-patterned upholstery fabric may show through. In that case, beige or a stripe may provide camouflage. Heavy white cotton duck is also opaque. Considering how cheap and easy working with sheets can be, it may make sense to make a couple of sets of slipcovers and change them with the seasons.

Other secret sources for very wide fabric—easy to wrap or cut for slipcovers and very, very cheap—are marine and theatrical suppliers. Muslin is a plain cotton weave available in natural

PALAZZETTI

Simon Intl.
Mantilla
sofa

28 yards

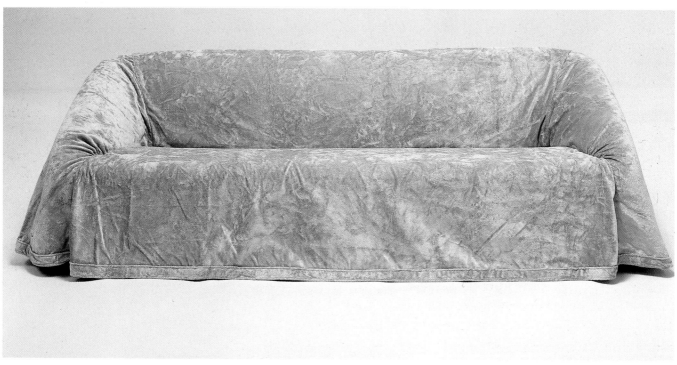

color only (though it's easy to dye), in widths up to 10 feet or more. Theater backdrops are painted on muslin or a very handsome natural linen 12 feet wide. Duck and sailcloth are two more heavy cottons that come in enormous widths. Duck is often available in pure white and colors, though it, too, can be dyed with some ease. Some really creative artists paint their own designs on duck or muslin with fabric paints for a truly custom cover.

Perhaps the greatest of all the many advantages of slipcovers is their moderate cost, since slipcover fabrics are lighter and therefore generally cheaper than upholstery fabrics. They are easy to make, keeping labor costs down. Of course, expensive material can be used, but even costly fabric can be bought on sale at department stores and outlets. Because slipcovers are usually inexpensive and temporary, they provide a chance to try out colors and fabrics much more unconventional than are normally used for upholstery. Happily, it's not a long-term commitment. A new set of slipcovers can be made as cheaply as the old one.

DOMAIN
Washable Posh™ *slipcovered sofa*

20 yards

YARDAGE IN SHEETS

For 44" wide fabric

CONVENTIONAL MEASUREMENTS			METRIC MEASUREMENTS	
Flat sheets	Finished Size	Approximate Yardage	Finished Size	Approximate Yardage
Twin	66" x 96"	4 yards	167cm x 243cm	3.7m
Double	81" x 96"	5 yards	205cm x 243cm	4.6m
Queen	90" x 102"	6 yards	228cm x 259cm	5.5m
King	108" x 102"	7 yards	274cm x 259cm	6.4m
Pillowcase, Standard	20" x 30"	2/3 yard	51cm x 76cm	.7m
Pillowcase, King	20" x 40"	1 yard	51cm x 101cm	.9m

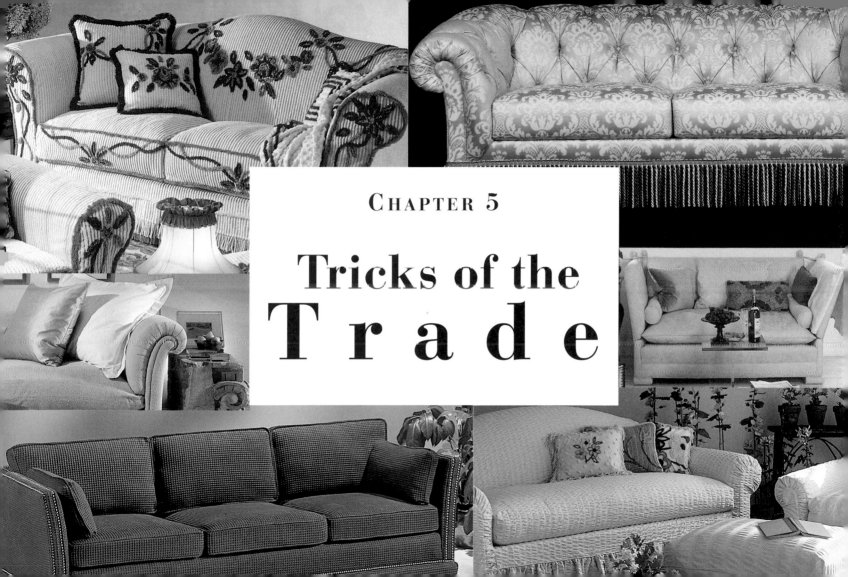

CHAPTER 5

Tricks of the
T r a d e

As every interior decorator knows, it's the details that count to give a room that finished "designer" look. Fortunately, the power to achieve the look is not limited to those who use a decorator or go to design school—each customer can play decorator when ordering a couch. Those special touches that give furniture its individuality and distinction are available from many large manufacturers, although the salesperson may need encouragement to get out all of the manufacturer's catalogs and do some telephoning to find out exactly what is offered.

∽ *The customer as decorator* ∽

Once the catalogs are spread out, it's important to make first those decisions that affect the shape of the couch. This is the time to specify the arm shape that has proven most comfortable as well as attractive.

Next comes the major decision about upholstery fabric. Before making a final choice, special arm and skirt detailing options should be taken into account. For instance, a "waterfall" arm detail (a full gathered front to soften the arm shape) looks far more graceful in a soft damask that will fall elegantly than in a stiff velvet or tapestry.

Finally, unusual trim options can be added for a truly custom look. Heavy four-inch *bullion fringe* in a matching or contrasting color around the base of the sofa is a stylish alternative to a fabric skirt. *Self-welting* (cording at the seams

covered with the upholstery fabric) can be replaced with a contrasting braid or rope trim. The skirt and/or cushions may be edged with braid or a band of contrasting fabric.

Before specifying one of these custom details, be sure that the manufacturer's finishing standards are very high. Other couches from the same company should have smoothly applied trim and well-matched fabric (see "The Material World," p. 95, for more on matching). Unevenly applied fancy trim will make the couch look amateurish, not stylish.

The ultimate decorator touch is providing the fabric and trim from outside sources, as discussed in the fabric chapter. However, using a stock material from the manufacturer will save time and probably money. That may make it cost-effective to splurge on custom details to individualize the upholstery and, as soon as possible, order a slipcover for a constantly available quick change.

A useful option to be ordered at the same time is a set of large polished-metal "Christmas

DREXEL
HERITAGE
1185 sofa
20.5 yards

ball" casters. Most manufacturers offer these large-diameter rollers at a small additional price. Because of their size and smooth finish, they don't damage carpeting like narrow casters and allow the sofa to be moved easily for cleaning. They blend well with metal-framed modern couches; on a traditional sofa they can be hidden under a skirt.

DREXEL
HERITAGE

*1182 love
sseat*

15.5 yards

⁓ Beautifying the basics ⁓

When buying an inexpensive basic couch whose manufacturer doesn't offer fancy options or when upgrading an old couch, it's not necessary to settle for a bargain-basement look. The first step is to add filling to cushions that arrive flat or have been flattened over the years. Upholstery stores sell filling materials for do-it-yourself work, or a local upholsterer should be able to fluff them up inexpensively. If the upholstery is too terrible, a slipcover with special trim touches, loose pillows and/or a throw will give a completely new look.

Henredon
H8864C
sofa
24 yards

⁓ Loose pillows ⁓

A lavish heap of pillows adds both comfort and style to a couch, whether it's a new purchase or an old faithful that is looking a bit tired. Interesting pillows can be found almost anywhere, in department stores or antiques shops or flea markets. Ethnic gift and clothing stores often carry unique pillows handcrafted in rural villages. Some adventurous people collect pillows on their

PILLOWS

Weltless
20" Square

Weltless
21" x 11½"

Knife-Edge
20" Square

Knife-Edge
20" Square

Weltless
13" x 27"

Weltless
18" Round

Box-Edge
15" Round

Ruffled
17" Square

travels, transforming a sofa into a decorative diary with happy associations. Homemade pillows in patchwork or needlepoint can be the most personal touch of all, wonderful reminders of important events in the lives of family and friends.

Whether plain or elaborate, pillows make seating furniture more comfortable. Everyone who will sit on the couch has a different shape and personality. A relatively short person will sit much more securely in a deep sofa when supported by a couple of pillows. Chatty folk often like to surround themselves with a cozy ring of pillows while passing on the finer points of a juicy story. And it's great, when reading, to have a pillow handy to prop up the book.

Many couches come with loose pillows in the same fabric as the upholstery. They are perfectly utilitarian, but certainly not stylish. They are useful as a background to more interesting pillows, or placed on an easy chair covered in a different

Simple stripes in a spectrum of colors add lively style to an informal room.

material. Department and furniture stores carry ready-made pillow covers in most standard sizes that are simply zipped over the existing pillow for an instant upgrade.

When covering loose pillows, using one fabric for all will provide contrast—a floral chintz with a solid pastel sofa, for instance. It's most important to be lavish with the number of extra pillows—an inviting heap of colors and shapes is the easiest of luxuries. Adding two pillows to the original pair is the absolute minimum, but more is better in this case. A variety of sizes and shapes gives extra visual interest: one long couch could hold a big down square that comes above the sofa back for relaxing, a couple of medium-size firm rectangles for support, and a shirred round or bolster just for the fun of it. And *please* don't line the pillows up across the back of the sofa and karate-chop them down the middle as is still occasionally done in ads for contract furniture. They're supposed to look welcoming, not aggressive.

Color demands the same imaginative approach as shape. Unless the room palette is a

pure monochrome, it's fun and very stylish to dress up the sofa with a collection of pillows in several fabrics and colors. This is the chance to combine needlepoint and velvet, old and new fabric, prints and plain colors. Scraps of old brocade or tapestry make wonderful pillows, as do pieces of flat-weave rugs which have worn too thin for the floor. Bits of precious lace can be applied to stronger fabrics to show off their delicate workmanship. Lustrous and expensive silks in delicate colors make delicious pillows. Gift shops often carry pillows shaped like what they represent—a cat, frog, butterfly or sunflower. Used sparingly, these can be charming, but too many cats or rabbits will make the room look like a nursery.

Pillows are a wonderful way to show off interesting trimmings, which are much easier to use and often more effective in small quantities (not to mention cheaper) than as a major part of the upholstery. The simplest trimming is welting, either matching or contrasting with the main fabric. Fancier choices are ruffles, cording and fringe. Some very complicated pillows may have

HENREDON
9164 sofa
18 yards

both lace ruffles and silk fringe. These are usually better suited to a boudoir than to the living room, but they can be very beautiful. Lots of fairly simply trimmed pillows may look wonderful together, but the more complex ones should be used with restraint.

The contrast of shapes, sizes, colors and textures of pillows is an expression of style and creativity. And nothing is easier than updating the couch in an instant with a new heap of pillows in fresh patterns and colors.

～ *Throws* ～

The next-easiest couch improver is a throw—a piece of woven cotton, wool, chenille or, for the truly fortunate, cashmere. A throw can be thrown temporarily over the sofa to brighten up the room or permanently to cover signs of wear or soiling.

The available choice of throws is vast and, even more than with pillows alone, has potential for instant makeovers. Draped on a basic beige couch, a printed cotton Indian bedspread looks casual and artistic, an Amish quilt somewhat formal but countryish, a fringed tapestry tablecloth festive. There's no reason not to use all these looks for different occasions and moods. A huge selection of throws, many of them both handsome and inexpensive, is to be found both in stores and in the many life-style catalogs that appear in the mail.

Throws are not simply decorative: they can double as cozy blankets for reading or napping. Soft cotton weaves based on early American coverlets are available in many patterns and colors at low prices. More expensive wool, cashmere or silk-and-cashmere blankets in neutrals or traditional plaids are luxurious to curl up in. Chenille is another soft, opulent fabric that comes in wonderful, natural colors. Chenille throws have long silky fringes and are a favorite accessory of many top decorators; they are suitable for any style of decoration and will add charm to the couch for a long time. With throws as with pillows, it's fun to experiment and change the look—every day if desired.

When imagining a throw, traditionalists will think instantly of a paisley shawl, deep in fringe,

DOMAIN

Washable Posh™ *slipcover sofa*

20 yards

strewn nobly over a velvet chesterfield. Velvet, in fact, is an ideal fabric over which to strew because the nap will hold other fabrics in place. Which brings up the only problem with throws. They do tend to slip around and, in extreme cases, fall right off the couch. The throw can be tucked around the cushions or anchored with upholstery pins, but it will still need to be straightened every time it has been sat on or against. Most people don't object to this, but it is something to keep in mind. A throw that has been left in a heap looks messy and sad.

ADVICE FROM THE EXPERTS

Some of America's most prestigious decorators have agreed to share the expertise about couches

CENTURY
22-610 sofa
18 yards

they've acquired through experience. They have very definite ideas, many of which can be adapted for any home. Among the subjects they discussed were their favorite fabrics, how to use trim and ways to customize and dress up a couch.

First of all, they emphasized, it's important to choose the right couch for the right place. Stanley Hura, who has designed custom couches for private clients and retail couches for the Pearson division of the Lane Company, insists that preliminary research (sitting on the couch, peeking under the cushions, pushing on the frame) is essential to be sure the couch is comfortable for the people who will sit in it, "*then* order custom details like extra pillows, trim on skirts, contrast welting." The retail companies are prepared to do custom work, he says, but it's the customer's responsibility to choose the best basic couch that fits the budget.

The prestigious New York architecture and design firm Shelton Mindel & Associates emphasizes choosing the right piece of furniture to complement the surroundings. They often use retail couches with custom details but, "it all depends on what the room dictates: piping, no piping, waterfall skirts, inlay bands of fabric or tape, new legs, no skirt, a fully upholstered platform base." As architects, they'll consider all sorts of styles and materials because "the sofa should be a synthesis of the architectural feeling and the function of the room."

Scale, too, is important. As Debra Blair of Shattuck Blair Associates points out, a big room requires an oversize sofa to be in proportion. Cushions can set the style—loose cushions give a casual look; tight ones, particularly on the back, are formal.

Vicente Wolf, a young interior designer who has designed upholstered furniture for Henredon, says the lines of the couch should be timeless, the construction sturdy. "You want a sofa that looks very designed but is classic so that everything else in the room can change around it and it will still look wonderful. Make sure it works from all angles—you may want to move it around."

An elegant couch benefits from down stuffing and pillows.

∾ *Comfort and luxury* ∾

VICENTE WOLF ASSOCIATES

With decorators, just like everyone else, comfort is a major consideration in choosing a couch. They have lots of ideas about how to make a couch as comfortable as possible. First among them is to order luxurious filling for the cushions. Most manufacturers offer foam-and-down or spring-and-down cushion filling at a moderate extra cost. It's well worth reaching to afford it—down pays back the investment in comfort every time it's sat on. These combination fillings don't require the same incessant fluffing as all-down, though they benefit from an occasional pat.

The more traditional and establishment the design firm, it seems, the more committed it is to pure down for sofa cushions. Libby Cameron of the quintessentially old-guard firm Parish-Hadley "likes down, all down. You'll get used to fluffing it." Vicente Wolf, goes even further. "I *like* the fluffing! I don't think people want their sofas to look perfect anymore—they like that almost messy look. I think there's nothing as wonderful as a down sofa that's all mushedlooking." Everyone who enjoys fluffing should order all-down cushions.

Other designers are less definite about down. Victoria Hagan of Feldman-Hagan in New York, advises clients to "pay the up-charge for down"—but suggests 80 percent polyfill/20 percent down for "soft cushions that don't need fluffing." Debra Blair says, "No one wants to deal with all-down seats." She, too, likes poly/down or foam core with down channels—options offered by the majority of manufacturers.

The firm of Shelton Mindel & Associates is not completely committed to down but won't get into the discussion of fluffing. They cite reasons of design appropriateness. "Some shapes don't look good in down" so they often use synthetic fillings to get the right effect. The streamlined modern designs so many architects love depend on high-density foam cushions for their clean lines.

Comfort is not only a matter of cushions. Mario Buatta, the Prince of Chintz, is also the king of comfort. He insists that sofas be "custom-made, hand-tied, down filled and stuffed with horsehair and all that. This is the best investment you're going to make . . . it should be of the highest quality and it should be *timeless, not trendy.*"

Stephanie Stokes, who has decorated some of the most elegant traditional residences in New York, feels that comfort comes from scaling the couch to the person. When ordering a custom sofa, she has the upholsterer vary the depth and tilt of the frame to fit the client, then uses custom webbing and filling to give that person his or her dream couch. Brian Brady of Brady McHugh Vaitkus in Philadelphia points out that it's easy to adjust the height of a retail couch by shortening or extending the legs to suit the height of the client. And Fred Clapper of Spitzer & Associates is thinking ahead: for an aging population, he recommends choosing a sofa with reasonably low arms to give support when sitting down and getting up. "After all," he says, "you will have a good sofa for twenty-five to fifty years and in time your ability to move changes."

❧ *Favorite fabrics* ❧

Looking at the more elaborate decorating magazines and show houses, one would be forgiven for thinking that the favorite fabric of top designers is silk brocade or linen velvet. But when asked, most of the designers showed a taste for the simple and practical.

Libby Cameron of Parish-Hadley is a fan of cotton duck because of its versatility. Canvas or duck slipcovers, especially in white, are favorites

JOHN
WIDDICOMB

*6376 Mario
Buatta Coll.
Alexandria
sofa*

24 yards

of many designers like Ann Dupuy of Holden & Dupuy in New Orleans, though Victoria Hagan of Feldman-Hagan in New York emphasizes that plain fabrics must *always* be stain-sealed, whether for upholstery or slipcovers.

Whatever the couch style, designers recommend ordering it *COM* (covered in the customer's own material—see "The Material World," page 95) to individualize the look. They select fabrics for their special qualities: Debra Blair likes

DOMAIN
Washable Posh™ slipcover sofa

20 yards

One key to a custom look, says Stanley Hura, is to use unexpected fabrics. He once upholstered a pale Shaker-style frame in black wool to give it a slightly shocking sophistication.

∾ *Details* ∾

Custom detailing adds the final decorator touch to a ready-made sofa. First of all, a decorator gets rid of the matching throw pillows or uses

RJONES
Cambridge sofa
17 yards

them on another piece of furniture. "Buy or make contrasting ones," says Victoria Hagan, "and vary the size and shape." She's also enthusiastic about finishing touches, particularly brass nailheads, which are available from most manufacturers, to accentuate the shape of the couch.

Contrast welting, shirred or bowed skirts, and inlaid bands of contrasting material or braid also personalize the couch. The manufacturer's detail charts of arm and skirts (like the ones on pages 123 and 124) can be mixed and matched; then, for a finishing touch, tassels or braid are added. Details like this will give the satisfaction of creating a unique couch without the trouble and expense of having it custom-made.

Though not a full-fledged decorator, the reader of this book is well on the way to making good decisions on how to buy a couch and what kind of a couch to buy. With a good working knowledge of style, inner structure and outer covering, all that remains is to find out where to get the sofa that, with luck, will give pleasure and comfort for years to come.

DREXEL
HERITAGE
1182 love seat

18 yards

WORKING WITH A DECORATOR

To make the best choice of a couch, is a decorator's advice essential? The fancy shelter magazines and many people will insist that it is. "Does a non-professional even know where to buy a couch?" they may ask. "How will you know if the price is right? Is the most expensive couch the best, and if so, why?" For many people, making such momentous decisions requires expert advice—which is why this book was written.

Nonetheless, working with a decorator has its advantages, most important in saving time. In an ideal designer/client relationship, the designer knows the client's taste and budget, and will scour "to-the-trade-only" sources on the client's behalf. He/she, having narrowed down the dizzying profusion of styles and fabrics offered in these secret showrooms, will then present a small selection of samples, each of which is more appealing and appropriate than the next. The client then makes the perfect selection and the decorator, having determined beforehand that the workroom is poised to begin, will specify exquisite finishing details to distinguish this couch from all others of similar configuration. Before the client even

begins to feel impatient, the perfect piece will take its place in the newly refurbished room—all within the original budget. That's the ideal.

In real life, the designer's understanding of a client's taste may be less than complete, or there may be pressure to conform to the decorator's own taste. After the the couch shape has been chosen from drawings or photos comes the decision whether synthetic filling will be soft enough or whether to indulge in *much* more expensive down cushions as the decorator suggests.

The client will be asked to select a fabric, but may find it hard to visualize the finished sofa while looking at a small swatch. Workrooms are often backed up, and even the promised 10- to 12-week delivery may stretch out to several months. When at last the sofa arrives, the pillows or the way the braid harmonizes with the fabric may not be quite as expected, but since it's a special order, it's nonreturnable.

The range of choice available to decorators is immense, but the success of the client/designer relationship rests on how well that choice is interpreted to the customer. Interpretation is what the client pays for, and it's sensible to remember that, in most cases, this includes at least two markups—one for the piece of furniture and one for the fabric. The custom workroom, too, may take a markup. The designer will presumably spend a good deal of time on the order, and the markups are usually part of his/her recompense. At the end of the project, a carefully planned budget may have disappeared in feathers and braid.

The secret of success is communication; even when working with a decorator, it will be easier to communicate clearly after reading this book. For the solo shopper, this book contains all the information needed to choose the best couch.

CENTURY
22-604 sofa
16 yards

CHAPTER 6

Where to Buy It

There are many ways to buy a couch: retail, wholesale, to-the-trade, auctions—among others. With such a selection, there's really no excuse for not finding the perfect couch.

Each type of source is explained below, along with some ways to gain access to to-the-trade showrooms. It's wise, when preparing to buy a rather expensive piece of furniture for the long term, to allot a considerable amount of time to studying the market. The study itself is most enjoyable as well as educational and may even be full of surprises. After learning about the many styles and constructions available in couches, the final choice may be very different from what you imagined at the outset.

FURNITURE MANUFACTURERS— RETAIL STORE SUPPLIERS

These are the department stores' suppliers. Although the consumer cannot buy directly from them, many are national advertisers. Their advertising strategy stimulates demand for their products, which are then marketed through the stores. Each advertisement carries an address or, more commonly, an 800 number for consumers to call to find the nearest retailer who carries the manufacturer's products. In some cases, the 800 number may refer only to the specific furniture in the advertisement, but the telephone marketer will give numbers for other products.

BAKER, KNAPP & TUBBS
917 Merchandise Mart
Chicago, IL 60604
(312) 329-9410

Traditional, reproduction and contemporary upholstery and fabrics. Collections include McMillen; Historic Charleston; Stately Homes of England, Scotland, Ireland; Charles Pfister; and the Hermitage Museum of St. Petersburg, Russia. Milling Road is a new, younger and less expensive line of informal furniture.

CENTURY FURNITURE CO.
P.O. Box 608
Hickory, NC 28603
(704) 328-1851

Collections of designer and reproduction upholstery from this large and varied company include Jay Spectre, Henry Ford Museum and Greenfield Village. The Sutton division makes meticulous reproductions from the collections of the Smithsonian Museum and the British National Trust.

DIRECTIONAL
P.O. Box 2005
High Point, NC 27261
(919) 841-3209

A strictly contemporary line of upholstery including many sectionals, which may be used for all kinds of configurations.

DREXEL HERITAGE
101 N. Main Street
Drexel, NC 28619
(919) 889-2501

Traditional and contemporary upholstery; collections include Biltmore Estate and American Themes.

HABERSHAM PLANTATION
P.O. Box 1209
Toccoa, GA 30577
(404) 886-1476

Traditional upholstery with a country flavor, rooted especially in the southern part of the U.S.

HARDEN FURNITURE CO.
Mill Pond Way
McConnellsville, NY 13401
(315) 245-1000

Traditional upholstery in classic styles; collections include Signatures and Country Inns.

HENREDON FURNITURE CO.
P.O. Box 70
Morganton, NC 28655
(704) 437-5261

Traditional and contemporary upholstery; collections include Historic Natchez.

HICKORY CHAIR CO.,
A DIVISION OF THE LANE CO.
P.O. Box 2147
Hickory, NC 28603
(704) 328-1801
Traditional upholstery collections, including James River, American Digest, Mark Hampton and the French Collection—reinterpretations of historic and designer furniture.

KINDEL FURNITURE CO.
P.O. Box 2047
Grand Rapids, MI 49501
(616) 243-3676
Traditional reproduction upholstery; collections include Winterthur, National Trust for Historic Preservation and Irish Georgian Society.

LALUNE COLLECTION
930 East Burleigh
Milwaukee, WI 53212
(414) 263-5300
Mission and twig-style benches, tables and upholstered furniture, often sold through catalogues.

LA-Z-BOY CHAIR CO.
1284 N. Telegraph
Monroe, MI 48161
(313) 242-1444
Traditional and contemporary upholstery, most famously including recliners and sofa beds. Styles have improved in recent years.

THE LANE COMPANY
P.O. Box 151
Alta Vista, VA 24517
(804) 369-5641
Traditional furniture, including Mission/Frank Lloyd Wright–style upholstery in the Grove Park Collection.

LEE INDUSTRIES
P.O. Box 26
Newton, NC 28658
(704) 464-8318
A large manufacturer of well-made traditional and contemporary upholstery in the medium price ranges.

LEXINGTON FURNITURE INDUSTRIES
P.O. Box 1008
Lexington, NC 27292
(704) 249-5300

Traditional and contemporary upholstery, including Lyn Hollyn at Home, Weekend Retreat and the phenomenally successful Bob Timberlake country collection.

LINEAGE HOME FURNISHINGS, INC.
P.O. Box 11188
High Point, NC 27265
(919) 454-6688

A traditional and contemporary furniture collection shown in special galleries within department and furniture stores.

MEYER-GUNTHER-MARTINI INC.,
AN AFFILIATE OF TROUVAILLES, INC.
64 Grove Street
Watertown, MA 02172
(617) 926-2520

Interpretations of eighteenth- and nineteenth-century French upholstered furniture with wooden and painted frames. Also to-the-trade.

HERMAN MILLER, INC.
Zeeland, MI 49464
(616) 772-3661

Contemporary upholstery, specializing in classic twentieth-century designs including those by Charles and Ray Eames and Eero Saarinen.

NATUZZI
P.O. Box 2438
High Point, NC 27261
(919) 887-8300

Contemporary leather upholstery specializing in Italian designs made accessible to American consumers.

PEARSON COMPANY,
A DIVISION OF THE LANE CO.
1420 Progress Street
High Point, NC 27261
(919) 882-8135

Traditional and contemporary upholstery collections, including America, Licensed by the Museum of American Folk Art (with designs by Stanley Hura) and Shaker Country.

PENNSYLVANIA HOUSE
Lewisburg, PA 17837
(717) 523-2155

A large variety of traditional upholstery in the medium price ranges, widely available throughout the country.

SOUTHWOOD REPRODUCTIONS
P.O. Box 2245
Hickory, NC 28603
(704) 465-1776

Eighteenth-century reproduction upholstery that is very accurate and very handsome.

STICKLEY
P.O. Box 480
Manlius, NY 13104
(315) 642-5500

Among the originators of Arts and Crafts style upholstery. Stickley originals are virtually priceless, but fortunately the company still produces many of its signature designs.

SWAIM
P.O. Box 4189
High Point, NC 27263
(919) 885-6131

Contemporary upholstery, designed in the main by John Mascheroni. It is classic in style and can easily be used in traditional interiors.

THAYER COGGIN
P.O. Box 5867
High Point, NC 27262
(919) 841-6000

A well-established manufacturer of contemporary upholstery that is widely available throughout the country.

THOMASVILLE FURNITURE IND., INC.
P.O. Box 339
Thomasville, NC 27361
(919) 472-2000

A wide range of traditional and contemporary furniture including the Country Inns and Back Roads Collection.

TROUVAILLES, INC.
64 Grove Sreet
Watertown, MA 02172
(617) 926-2520
Line-for-line reproductions of French, English and continental furniture from the seventeenth-century through Art Deco, including Biedermeier and Russian collections. Also to-the-trade.

JOHN WIDDICOMB CO.
601 Fifth Street N.W.
Grand Rapids, MI 49504
(616) 459-7173
Traditional upholstery; collections include Mario Ruatta, Russian and English.

FURNITURE MANUFACTURERS— TO-THE-TRADE

The most difficult to approach of all sources for furniture and fabrics are the showrooms that deal only with the design trades. Most are located in special design buildings where consumers may not even be allowed past the front door. The reason for this is that the products are sold at a discount—usually 30 to 40 percent off retail—to-the-trade. Decorators and architects add a markup of from 10 percent to full retail when selling to the client. The showrooms wish to protect the trade markup and feel it is none of the consumer's business to know the trade price. Even within the showrooms, prices are usually marked in one of a number of codes, and the true price will rarely be quoted to a consumer. Naturally, many people are convinced that these are the most desirable of sources and thrive on the challenge of gaining access.

In fact, many retail sources from department stores to decorator shops offer the same products or ones of equal quality, so it is not necessary to infiltrate the design centers to buy good furniture or fabrics. However, it's always interesting to find out what is available and there are ways to get into the showrooms.

Many of the "to-the-trade-only" showrooms in design buildings will, in fact, allow the public to enter when they are not too busy. A brand-new, consumer-friendly trend is the establishment of retail buying services in many design buildings. Personnel from these services—usually trained designers—will accompany consumers into the showrooms and place orders for one or two items at an agreed markup that may be less than retail; for more extensive jobs the buying offices usually have a decorator referral service.

For a consumer who prefers to go it alone, a quiet but confident approach will almost always meet with success. It's a help to be able to produce a business card from a designer friend since the majority of showrooms allow clients to enter.

Some showrooms will let a client enter only if accompanied by the decorator; there are a few super-tough establishments from which the public is barred with or without a designer.

Once inside the showroom, take time to go through the wings on which the fabric is displayed and look carefully at the furniture. It's useful to see the fabric in long lengths rather than swatches and to be able to sit on a couch. Noting choices by pattern name and number saves time with a decorator or prepares you to deal with a factory outlet. Chances of placing an order directly are slim, though it's worth a try. Some showrooms have started to deal with the public at retail prices, on the logical theory that the showroom, rather than the decorator, should profit from the markup.

Furniture ordered from a showroom is priced in muslin—the upholstery fabric is bought and paid for separately. It may come from the same showroom or be delivered from another source, so you will need to know the yardage requirement. Delivery may be as long as eight to ten weeks.

Listed are the flagship showrooms of many furniture manufacturers. Others may be found in the design centers. Usually their products are distributed nationwide in either their own showrooms or by representatives. A phone call will get you the name of the nearest source.

ARC INTERNATIONAL, INC.
91 Fifth Avenue
New York, NY 10003
(212) 727-3340

Contemporary upholstery, including the Patrick Naggar collection of French furniture.

ARKITEKTURA
379 West Broadway
Fourth Floor
New York, NY 10012
(212) 334-5570

Contemporary upholstery from a showroom that is also open to the public. Designers include Geoffrey Beene, Michael Graves and Eero Saarinen.

ATELIER INTERNATIONAL, LTD.
IDCNY Center 2
30–20 Thompson Avenue
Long Island City, NY 11101
(718) 392-0300

Contemporary upholstery, specializing in classic twentieth-century designs and furniture from modern icons like Le Corbusier, Mackintosh, Rietveld and the designers of the Memphis Group.

B & B ITALIA
IDCNY Center 2 , Space 401
30–40 Thompson Avenue
Long Island City, NY 11101
(718) 784-0211

Contemporary upholstery from Italy by leading designers including Afra and Tobias Scarpa, Gaetano Pesce, Paolo Piva and Mario Bellini.

BRUNSCHWIG & FILS, INC.
75 Virginia Road
White Plains, NY 10603
Showroom: 979 Third Avenue
New York, NY 10022.
(212) 838-7878

Traditional upholstery of luxurious design that can be ordered from the showroom covered in any of the many fine fabrics for which Brunschwig is primarily known.

DIALOGICA
484 Broome Street
New York, NY 10013
(212) 966-1934

Romantic modern designs by Monique and Sergio Savarese in sleek contemporary style.

DONGHIA FURNITURE/TEXTILES
485 Broadway
New York, NY 10013
(212) 925-2777

Very elegant contemporary upholstery pieces that can be used effectively in traditional rooms. They may be covered in the firm's own line of fabrics, particularly Donghia's signature beige–and–white striped linen.

GRANGE FURNITURE
200 Lexington Avenue
New York, NY 10016
(212) 685-9057

Traditional French upholstery in a number of styles from a retro-Fifties huge chesterfield to more predictable country-inspired settees.

HaRry
8639 Venice Boulevard
Los Angeles, CA 90034
(310) 559-7863

Contemporary upholstery, specializing in combinations of vinyl and fabrics in pop culture–inspired wild west/space age color mixtures and trims. Also retail.

ICF, INC.
305 East 63rd Street
Seventh Floor
New York, NY 10021
(212) 750-0900

Contemporary upholstery, specializing in classic twentieth-century designs.

RJONES & ASSOCIATES., INC.
P.O. Box 560705
Dallas, TX 75356
(214) 951-0095

Contemporary upholstery in classic styles that can usefully be combined with traditional elements.

KNOLL INTERNATIONAL
655 Madison Avenue
New York, NY 10021
(212) 207-2200

Contemporary upholstery and fabric, specializing in classic twentieth-century designs including Sotsass, Charles Pfister and Mies van der Rohe's leather seating.

LIGNE ROSET USA
200 Lexington Avenue
New York, NY 10016
(212) 685-2238

Interpretations of some of the high-style upholstery ideas of France's leading designers—but more accessible and affordable.

MEYER-GUNTHER-MARTINI INC.,
AN AFFILIATE OF TROUVAILLES, INC.
64 Grove Street
Watertown, MA 02172
(617) 926-2520

Interpretations of eighteenth- and nineteenth-century French upholstered furniture with wooden and painted frames.

NEOTU
133 Greene Street
New York, NY 10012
(212) 982-0210

Contemporary upholstery manufactured in France. Designers Garouste and Bonetti are represented here, as well as innovative Americans. Also retail.

PALAZZETTI

515 Madison Avenue

New York, NY 10022

(212) 832-1177

Contemporary upholstery, specializing in classic twentieth-century designs.

THE SHARPE NICHOLS COMPANY

6452 East Fulton Street

Ada, MI 49301

(616) 676-5960

A company specializing in Deco-inspired leather upholstery.

TROUVAILLES, INC.

64 Grove Street

Watertown, MA 02172

(617) 926-2520

Line-for-line reproductions of English, French and continental furniture from the seventeenth century through Art Deco. Collections include Russian and Biedermeier.

FURNITURE RETAILERS— DEPARTMENT STORES

One result of the demise of big furniture stores like W & J Sloane in the New York area has been the expansion of department store furniture selections in downtown and mall locations. A lot of money and energy has been expended to make these departments appealing. The leading role is currently being played by self-contained boutiques featuring such upmarket designers as Ralph Lauren and Mario Buatta. Historic reproductions from Williamsburg, Charleston or the Stately Homes of England are grouped next to areas devoted to Shaker, Neo-Deco or Santa Fe styles.

The advantage of department store shopping is in the opportunity to compare styles as well as the chance to sit in the precise piece of furniture, often covered in the exact fabric, that you will buy. When choosing from the fabric selection offered with the couch, large sample pieces are available to try on the furniture. Usually department stores have fabric departments from which customers can select materials besides those supplied by the couch manufacturer. Where style is concerned, manufacturers offer many modifications—usually including skirt style, trim and cushion filling, as discussed in Chapter 5. Delivery time is usually six to eight weeks when the furniture is being covered from the manufacturer's stock. The couch may also be ordered COM (upholstered in your own material) but delivery may take longer. Many stores have in-house decorating departments where interior designers are available to give advice about both fabric and decorator details. They may even be able to order from to-the-trade fabric showrooms.

A department store normally charges full retail price. However, furniture goes on sale regularly, with the deepest discounts traditionally in January and July/August. If you find the perfect sofa in a suitable fabric, it may be possible to buy it in a floor sample sale. It will almost always be dramatically reduced—just be sure to weigh the wear and tear of being on display against the use it would have had in the same period at home.

Department stores advertise regularly in local newspapers. This is the best way to find out about the stores in nearby towns and malls, and about the timing of their sales. The recent spate of bankruptcies has sadly depleted the number of department stores; in any case few are truly national, with the exception of:

Macy's

Nordstrom

Bloomingdale's

K mart

J. C. Penney

Sears, Roebuck & Co.

FURNITURE RETAILERS— STORES AND CATALOGS

National home furnishings chains such as Conran's, IKEA and Pier 1 carry sofas and sofa beds along with the components of a rather unpretentious life-style, from dhurrie rugs to duvet covers. Many of them sell from mail-order catalogs as well. Couch styles are usually at the modern end of the classic spectrum. The look is stylish and the prices low, reflecting relatively light-duty construction. Furniture is kept in stock and can be carried home or delivered within a few days. Couches from these sources, which are sold as shown without modifications, are best chosen for short-term use. They will serve faithfully until an upgrade becomes possible.

Other home furnishings stores such as Ethan Allen and Expressions are really retail showrooms for one manufacturer's products. They display high-quality furniture as it might be arranged in a home, with coordinated accessories to complete the look. The style is too homogeneous for most people, but it's a help to see how each couch fits into a room setting. Pieces chosen from these stores are well-made and built to last. Some modifications are possible. Delivery time is usually short.

Like department stores, home furnishings stores charge full retail, but they, too, have periodic sales and floor-sample clearances.

Catalogs are a fact of American life. Many of the glossy publications that pour out of the mail include upholstered furniture. Some, like Crate & Barrel, have stores in a few localities; others, like the ubiquitous Horchow, are strictly mail order. All will answer questions over the telephone and send fabric swatches.

ABC CARPET & HOME
888 Broadway
New York, NY 10003
(212) 473-3000
Antique and reproduction upholstery imported from around the world—mostly in country styles. Some contemporary collections.

ETHAN ALLEN INC.
P.O. Box 1966
Danbury, CT 06813
(203) 743-8000
International home furnishings company carrying traditional and contemporary styles. Upholstery in fabric and leather. Over 300 Ethan Allen Home Interiors stores throughout the United States, Canada and abroad.

ARCHETYPE
37 Spring Street
New York, NY 10012
(212) 334-0100

Contemporary furniture, mostly from young and often funky designers.

ARKITEKTURA
379 West Broadway
Fourth Floor
New York, NY 10012
(212) 334-5570

Contemporary upholstery in a showroom that is also open to the public. Designers include Geoffrey Beene, Michael Graves and Eero Saarinen.

EDDIE BAUER HOME COLLECTION
P.O. Box 3700
Seattle, WA 98124
(800) 426-8020

A catalog of outdoor wear that has branched out into upholstered furniture of a classic traditional style, generally most suitable for informal or country-style interiors.

CARLYLE CUSTOM CONVERTIBLES, LTD.
1056 Third Avenue
New York, NY 10021
(212) 838-1525

Manufacturer of mostly traditional upholstered furniture. Pieces can be bought as seen on the floor of the showroom or ordered in a wide selection of styles, fillings, fabrics and trims, with or without convertibility.

CHOICE SEATING GALLERY
(212) 598-4155

Forty-five locations in the East selling 500 styles of sofas, sectionals and sleepers in a choice of over 3,000 fabrics and 250 leathers.

THE COMPANY STORE
500 Company Store Road
LaCrosse, WI 54601
(800) 323-8000

Although mainly a supplier of pillows, comforters and other bedding, this catalog also offers futons, frames and covers.

CONRAN'S HABITAT
(800) 3-CONRAN

An international group of stores selling well-designed contemporary furniture, which is most suitable for short-term uses at low prices. Call the 800 number for the nearest store. A catalog is sent periodically.

CRATE & BARREL
(800) 323-5461

New England retail and outlet stores with a national catalog. Upholstered furniture lines in simple classic style are being expanded.

DIALOGICA
484 Broome Street
New York, NY 10013
(212) 966-1934

Romantic modern designs by Monique and Sergio Savarese in sleek contemporary style.

DOMAIN, INC.
51 Morgan Drive
Norwood, MA 02062
(800) 888-1388

With 12 stores on the East Coast, Domain carries a wide range of traditional and contemporary designs including a slipcover collection.

THE DOOR STORE
1 Park Avenue
New York, NY 10016
(800) 433-4071

Thirteen stores in New York, Conneticut and New Jersey, offering a full line of moderately priced traditional and contemporary upholstery with a selection of fabrics.

EXPRESSIONS CUSTOM FURNITURE
3212 West Esplanade
Metairie, LA 70002
(800) 544-4519

A national chain selling only custom upholstery in over 150 frame styles and more than 600 fabric choices in which each can be covered.

HaRry
8639 Venice Boulevard
Los Angeles, CA 90034
(310) 559-7863

Contemporary upholstery, specializing in combinations of vinyl and fabrics in pop culture–inspired wild west/space age color mixtures and trims. Also to-the-trade.

HORCHOW HOME COLLECTION
P.O. Box 819069
Dallas, TX 75381-9069
(800) 456-7000

This, like others of the many Horchow catalogs, includes an ever-growing selection of rather traditional upholstered furniture. Fabric swatches available.

IKEA, INC.
Plymouth Commons
Plymouth Meeting, PA 19462
(215) 834-0872

National retailer of contemporary and traditional upholstery at amazingly low prices considering the good design. Construction is light. Yearly catalogs.

JENNIFER CONVERTIBLES
(800) JENNIFER

National retailer of convertible and standard sofas and love seats in many styles and fabrics. Good sale reductions.

RALPH LAUREN HOME COLLECTION
1185 Avenue of the Americas
New York, NY 10036
(212) 642-8729

Traditional upholstery sold primarily through Ralph Lauren galleries in department stores.

MORPHEUS FUTON & HOME FURNISHINGS
309 East 9th Street
New York, NY 10003
(212) 505-2691

Hardwood frames—maple is preferred. Futons are made of long-staple white cotton in tight-weave cotton ticking. Futon covers and other furniture are sold in the store.

NEOTU
33 Greene Street
New York, NY 10012
(212) 982-0210

Contemporary upholstery manufactured in France. Designs from Garouste and Bonetti, as well as innovative Americans. Also to-the-trade.

PALAZZETTI
515 Madison Avenue
New York, NY 10022
(212) 832-1199

Contemporary upholstery, specializing in classic twentieth-century European designs. Exclusive importers of Alivar fine reproductions of modern icons. Also the Maverick collection of young American designers' furniture.

PIER 1 IMPORTS
(800) 447-4371

Furniture and accessories at good prices, mostly in casual country style. Many sales.

GEORGE SMITH SOFAS AND CHAIRS, INC.
67–73 Spring Street
New York, NY 10012
(212) 226-4747

Traditional Victorian upholstery with an English club feel; the fabrics are imported and the couches are typically upholstered in kilim rug–style geometric designs or soft, almost faded-looking floral linens.

STURBRIDGE YANKEE WORKSHOP
P.O. Box 4000
Westbrook, ME 04098
(800) 426-8020

Very traditional Early American style couches in a small selection of fabrics are offered by this widely distributed catalog.

FURNITURE RETAILERS— DISCOUNT

Buying from a factory outlet or discounter is an excellent idea for the person who has made a definite selection of a couch (or any other piece of furniture, of course). The savings are substantial and the outlets have access to virtually every U.S. manufacturer. They typically have few pieces in stock but order from the manufacturer in the same way as any other retailer. Waiting time is essentially the same, as well. They deliver and perform any setting-up services needed, often at no additional cost. There is, however, no return or cancellation on a couch ordered this way, as it is a special order.

These outlets advertise widely in newspapers and in the back of decorating magazines and the yellow pages. Some of the discounters have shops, mainly in big cities or in the furniture-manufacturing centers of the South. Even though many people refer to these outlets as "the 800 numbers," those in North Carolina have local numbers due to a law pushed through by the regular retailers who felt the competition was unfair. When an out-of-stater calls, a salesperson takes the number and calls back immediately. The store sends out a brochure outlining the conditions of sale before finalizing an order. For nervous customers, most will provide references.

It's best and easiest to have the exact stock number of the piece of furniture when shopping these outlets. Some of the telephone sources require it. The place to find the manufacturer's stock number is in the department store or showroom on a hang tag attached to the couch. It's important, when writing down numbers, to note the name and dimensions as well. Although the store hang tag may not identify the manufacturer, there's usually a label on the frame or under the seat cushions.

Armed with as much information as possible, get in touch with discount outlets. It sometimes turns out that the number on the tag is the store's (rather than the manufacturer's) identification. In that case the name and dimensions may save the day. Quite often the knowledgeable people on the other end of the telephone can identify the couch from a good verbal description and will send photographs for verification. Others will send manufacturers' complete catalogs. Once the exact sofa is agreed upon, a price and delivery date will be quoted on the telephone. The store will send a confirmation that becomes an order on their receipt of your deposit of between 25 and 75 percent of the final price. Some take credit cards, others demand a certified check or money order on delivery.

Outlet prices are always good, but the greatest savings may be found on discontinued furniture styles. Since the point is to save money by expending time and energy, it makes sense to call more than one outlet. Prices and availability may vary quite substantially.

All of the outlets listed have furniture from a wide selection of manufacturers. It is necessary to call them with the stock number of the desired piece, and they will reply as to availability.

FURNITURE SHOWCASE OF
HIGH POINT, INC.
214 N. Main Street
P.O. Box 2327
High Point, NC 27261
(919) 884-1218

HOLTON FURNITURE CO.
805 Randolph Street
P.O. Box 280
Thomasville, NC 27361
(919) 472-0400

MALLORY'S FINE FURNITURE
2153 Lejeune Boulevard
P.O. Box 1150
Jacksonville, NC 28541
(919) 353-1828

NORTH CAROLINA DISCOUNT
FURNITURE SALES
3200 Clarendon Bouelvard
New Bern, NC 28563
(919) 638-9164

NORTH CAROLINA FURNITURE
SHOWROOMS
12 West 21st Street
Second Floor
New York, NY 10010
(212) 645-2524

SHELL INTERIORS LTD.
149–56 14th Avenue
Queens, NY 11357
(718) 767-3700

UTILITY CRAFT
2630 Eastchester Drive
High Point, NC 27265
(919) 454-6153

VILLAGE FURNITURE HOUSE
146 West Avenue
Kannapolis, NC 28081
(704) 938-9171

FURNITURE RETAILERS— DECORATOR SHOPS

A new variety of home furnishings shop is becoming popular around the country. It's a hybrid between a decorator source and a retail store. Usually founded by designers who wish to deal with a wider public, stores like Charlotte Moss or Anne Mullin offer antiques, exclusive decorative pieces and upholstered furniture made to their own designs. Couches and chairs are covered in their own workrooms in fabrics usually available only through decorators. One of the great advantages in buying from this sort of shop is that you have the decorator's privilege of changing skirt style, piping, trim and sometimes even the shape of an arm. Delivery may be slow if the workroom is busy.

These shops have decorating departments that will modify a couch, help select a fabric or lamp shade or design an entire house. Decorator shops are not inexpensive, but offer custom service as needed. Very occasional sales may produce bargains. New decorator shops open frequently; they usually advertise in local papers.

F. F. & E
437 Hayes Street
San Francisco, CA 94122
(415) 703-0718

Vintage modernist and craft furniture, as well as Dialogica upholstery from New York. Custom commissions and design advice offered.

IRELAND PAYS
2428 Main Street
Santa Monica, CA 90405
(310) 396-5035

Decorating and exclusive accessories with an English flavor. By appointment only.

CHARLOTTE MOSS & CO.
1027 Lexington Avenue
New York, NY 10021
(212) 772-3320

An elegant shop selling upholstered furniture designed by Ms. Moss; fabric, especially England's prestigious Colefax & Fowler collections (otherwise available only to-the-trade); custom accessories, decorative antiques, books, etc. A complete decorating service is available.

ANNE MULLIN INTERIORS
289 Greenwich Avenue
Greenwich, CT 06830
(203) 625-0184

Three stores in lower New England, offering everything from upholstery, antiques and accessories to a full decorating service. Brunschwig & Fils decorator fabrics are featured.

NEW AMERICAN COUNTRY
14 Post Road East
Westport, CT 06880
(203) 454-1002

Exclusive upholstered furniture in traditional and casual styles that can be covered in fabric or leather. Design service.

LORI PONDER, LTD.
5221 Wisconsin Avenue, N.W.
Washington, DC 20015
(202) 537-1010

Traditional English-style upholstery with a manor house slant: the Lori Ponder classical seating line as well as other designer offerings. Imported fabrics from England and France.

SLATKIN & CO.
131 East 70th Street
New York, NY 10021
(212) 794-1661

A shop full of furniture and accessories including exclusive upholstery in traditional English style and imported fabrics. Decorating service available.

Fabric Manufacturers— To-the-Trade

These manufacturers—like the furniture makers—sell only to decorators and architects through nationwide networks of showrooms in design centers. They are considered the top of the field in fabrics. The tactics discussed for gaining admittance to furniture showrooms may also work for fabrics. Although the showrooms will never admit it, some of their fabrics can sometimes be found at telephone and retail discounters. A selection of the best-known showrooms is included here, and many more will be found in the design buildings.

ROBERT ALLEN FABRICS
253 Ridgewood Drive
Rockey Hill, CT 06067
(800) 333-3777

BRUNSCHWIG & FILS, INC.
75 Virginia Road
White Plains, NY 10603
Showroom: 979 Third Avenue
New York, NY 10022
(212) 838-7878

Expensive and beautiful traditional fabric. This firm has a huge selection of all sorts of prints and wovens. It is most famous for its chintzes and for reproductions and reinterpretations of historic documents including Winterthur.

MANUEL CANOVAS
979 Third Avenue
New York, NY 10022
(212) 752-9588

A large collection of fabrics from France including many wovens but best known for large-scale prints in bright colors.

CLARENCE HOUSE IMPORTS
979 Third Avenue
New York, NY 10022
(212) 752-2890

Mostly traditional fabrics from England, France and Italy. Prints, chintzes, wovens and silks in great profusion make up their mostly expensive stock.

COWTAN & TOUT
979 Third Avenue
New York, NY 10022
(212) 753-4488

Traditional fabrics of all sorts, including their own exclusive designs and the full collections of Colefax & Fowler of England.

ROSE CUMMINGS CHINTZES, LTD.
252 East 59th Street
New York, NY 10022
(212) 888-2837

Many famous chintz patterns beloved of decorators for two generations are to be found here. A specialty is designs including roses.

DONGHIA FURNITURE / TEXTILES
485 Broadway
New York, NY 10013
(212) 925-2777

Contemporary fabric. Specializes in wovens for covering the most sophisticated contemporary furniture. Angelo Donghia, the founder, made beige-and-white striped linen popular for upholstery.

FONTHILL LTD.
979 Third Avenue
New York, NY 10022
(212) 755-6700

A fairly small but very beautiful line of exclusive silks and handprints in addition to the Pierre Frey collections from France.

CHRISTOPHER HYLAND INC.
979 Third Avenue
New York, NY 10022
(212) 688-6121

Imported English fabric including Watts & Co., Gainsborough Silk Weavers and Timney-Fowler.

KNOLL INTERNATIONAL
655 Madison Avenue
New York, NY 10021
(212)207-2200

Contemporary fabrics, mainly textures and wovens suitable for covering high-style contemporary furniture.

JACK LENOR LARSEN
41 East 11th Street
New York, NY 10003
(212) 674-3993

One of the pioneers of creative weaving, this firm specializes in elegant textures woven of natural fibers in earth colors.

LEE/JOFA
800 Central Park Boulevard
Carlstadt, NJ 07072
(201) 438-8444

One of the great suppliers of a full range of upholstery fabrics. Many English chintzes, such as the fern design beloved of pioneering decorator Elsie de Wolfe, come from this house.

OSBORNE & LITTLE, INC.
979 Third Avenue
New York, NY 10022
(212) 751-3333

An English manufacturer of mainly traditional cotton prints, wovens and silks. Their showrooms also carry the Nina Campbell, Designers Guild and Fardis collections.

CHRISTOPHER NORMAN INC.
979 Third Avenue
New York, NY 10022
(212) 644-4100

This showroom carries upholstered furniture as well as fabrics, but is best known for an exclusive line of silk stripes, plains and patterns.

ARTHUR SANDERSON & SONS
979 Third Avenue
New York, NY 10022
(212) 319-7220

Although they carry a selection of prints and wovens for upholstery, this firm is best known as the source for the original William Morris fabrics, cornerstone of the Arts and Crafts movement in England. They are still produced from the original rollers and hand-printing blocks.

SCALAMANDRE
300 Trade Zone Drive
Ronkonkoma, NY 11779
(516) 467-8800

This prestigious, old, family-owned silk-weaving firm specializes in making many of the special reproduction fabrics used in historic houses and the White House. Much of the silk is woven and their fabulous trimming tied in their New York factory. The fabrics are mostly very expensive but they own outlet stores in the New York area called Silk Surplus, where amazing bargains in fabric and trimming often can be found.

F. SCHUMACHER & CO.
79 Madison Avenue
New York, NY 10016
(212) 213-7900

Manufacturers of an extremely large selection of all kinds of fabrics for upholstery. Schumacher also produces the Waverly fabrics that are sold in retail stores.

FABRIC—RETAIL AND DISCOUNT

Many fabric outlets—Calico Corner is probably the biggest—have shops in malls and cities around the country. Some of the fabric outlets deal by mail order. Their selections are large and it is sometimes surprising to find that material supposedly sold to the trade only is available, especially through the telephone services. Prices are often much lower than the decorator cost. However, fabric may have been sold to an outlet because it is slightly off in color. When trying to match a particular pattern, it is best to take or send a swatch.

Small fabric retailers and discounters are often found in malls and through advertisements in local newspapers.

LAURA ASHLEY
1300 MacArthur Boulevard
Mahwah, NJ 07430
(800) 847-0202

English traditional fabrics sold mainly through Laura Ashley Home stores. Another collection is sold through retailers nationally.

CALICO CORNERS
203 Gale Lane
Kennett Square, PA 19348
(215) 444-9700

Seventy-five stores across the country offer a wide selection of domestic and imported fabrics at great savings.

DAMPIERRE & CO.
79 Greene Street
New York, NY 10003
(212) 966-5474

Imported French fabrics including large, bold contemporary prints and traditional designs.

THE DECORATOR'S OUTLET
(800) 253-9508

Telephone discounter of first-quality designer fabrics.

THE FABRIC CENTER
485 Electric Avenue
Fitchburg, MA 01420
(508) 343-4402

Discount traditional and contemporary fabric through a mail-order catalog.

RALPH LAUREN HOME COLLECTION
1185 Avenue of the Americas
New York, NY 10036
(212) 642-8729

Traditional-style fabrics sold primarily through Ralph Lauren galleries in department stores.

MARLENE'S DECORATOR FABRICS
301 Beech Street
Hackensack, NJ 07601
(800) 992-7325

Telephone discounter that will try to get any fabric from any manufacturer at a low cost.

RAINTREE DESIGNS
979 Third Avenue
New York, NY 10022
(212) 477-8590

Manufacturers of English-style Victoria Morland fabrics that are nationally distributed at retail.

SILK SURPLUS
235 East 58th Street
New York, NY 10022
(212) 753-6511

*An extraordinary outlet owned by the extremely
expensive to-the-trade Scalamandre company.
Amazing bargains in fabric and trimmings are
available, especially during their periodic sales.*

GEORGE SMITH SOFAS AND CHAIRS, INC.
67–73 Spring Street
New York, NY 10012
(212) 226-4747

*English fabrics from the respected firm of Bennison.
Their specialty is linen printed in soft, almost
faded-looking colors for an aristocratic, country-
house look.*

WAVERLY
79 Madison Avenue
New York, NY 10016
(212) 213-7900

*Traditional fabrics distributed nationally in
department and home improvement stores.*

THRIFT AND JUNK SHOPS

Hospitals and other charitable institutions operate thrift shops, where it is sometimes possible to find good, serviceable furniture that needs only re-covering to come back to life. The Salvation Army has been a famous source of recyclable furniture for generations, as have secondhand or "junk" shops where the contents of entire houses are sold off at a fraction of their value.

Inspect secondhand furniture carefully to be sure the frame is not cracked or the springs sprung. The couch, to be a true bargain, must be in sound condition. On the other hand, worn upholstery is relatively easy to replace and pillows can be plumped up with fresh feathers or synthetic filling, as explained in the previous chapters.

Before buying a secondhand "bargain," it's only sensible to know the price of a new sofa that answers your needs. Reupholstery and freshening of cushions is not cheap. You could get very lucky and find a sofa needing only a slipcover. If so, don't pass it up.

Thrift and junk shops are listed in yellow pages and may advertise.

AUCTIONS

Auctions are potential bargain sources. But beware! It's important to inspect the piece before getting caught up in the heady competition of bidding. Many overenthusiastic bidders have lived to regret their auction triumphs. Auction houses put sale lots on exhibit, usually a few days before the sale, allowing prospective buyers to inspect the pieces. If bidding in person is inconvenient or too intimidating, the auction house will usually accept a written bid. If the written bid prevails, they will call the bidder after the sale.

The press is full of stories about the two leading auction houses, Christie's and Sotheby's, where furniture and works of art change hands for millions of dollars. However, there are many less-high-powered auction houses selling off mainly the contents of estates, and even the two giants have sales of decorative (which means relatively inexpensive) furniture from time to time.

One popular weekend amusement is the country auction, which is often announced by flyers posted in grocery stores and on trees locally. Country auctions are also advertised in local papers and in *Maine Antiques Digest,* a newspaper serving dealers and collectors.

This list covers the New York City area; most cities have auction houses where estate sales take place. This is the sort of auction that is most likely to produce good, serviceable furniture at a reasonable price.

CHRISTIE'S FINE ART AUCTIONEERS
502 Park Avenue
New York, NY 10022
(212) 546-1000
The flagship American venue for this auction gallery. However, bargains may be found even here by the knowledgeable. Christie's auctions are held in several locations in the United States on occasion.

CHRISTIE'S EAST
219 East 67th Street
New York, NY 10021
(212) 606-0400

The auctions of less rare and less expensive but still desirable decorative pieces take place at this location regularly. Prices are often very good.

WILLIAM DOYLE GALLERIES INC.
175 East 87th Street
New York, NY 10128
(212) 427-2730

Regular auctions of mainly decorative pieces, though some fine furniture makes its way here.

LUBIN GALLERIES
30 West 26th Street
New York, NY 10010
(212) 924-3777

With Tepper (below), one of the houses auctioning mainly estate furniture. Bargains may be found in serviceable but out-of-date pieces.

SOTHEBY'S
1334 York Avenue
New York, NY 10021
(212) 606-7000

One of the two most important auction houses where great art is sold. However, decorative sales here may yield bargains.

TEPPER GALLERIES INC.
110 East 25th Street
New York, NY 10010
(212) 677-5300

An auction house selling only decorative furniture, mainly the contents of apartments and houses in the New York area. For someone with time to check the exhibitions regularly there are many bargains to be found.

INDEX